3/8/03
Come back soon —
Come back often... Portland's
gain is our loss — The Mariners

GOD WHOSE GOING TO
COVER ME IN THE
NEIGHBOR PARTIES!
BEST WISHES COME VISIT.
LOVE Chortiss

Charly! Two big 101
flunked English —
(see above) — you've
We'll miss you all - you've
been awesome neighbors
and great friends —
Can't wait to visit
Portland!
The Suchets

Cheers! Boise
Remember
@ Sun Valley! We'll
have more happy times,
See you in the summer.
Laurie
+ Mike
Fitzpatrick

Thanks for the memories

To the Kerry family,
Best of luck in
Portland. We'll
miss you dearly!
Thanks for
being such
great neighbors
Denise +
Steve Fuchs

We'll miss you, but
not as much as the
Dixie chicks. Hope
to see you both in
Portland + here.
It was great getting
to know you.
The Longs

I just don't know what we will do without you... our social lives will suffer greatly. We wish you all the best in Oregon and thanks for being such wonderful neighbors.

You will be missed.

The Fords
Jim, Chandy
Jack & Andy

Seasons of
BOISE

The Boise Metro Chamber of Commerce and Community Communications, Inc. would like to express our gratitude to the following companies for their leadership in the development of this book.

Seasons of
BOISE

By Colleen Birch Maile

Featuring the photography of
David Frazier, Patrick Teglia, Steve Bly, Chad Case, and Troy Maben

Corporate profiles by Jim Dunham

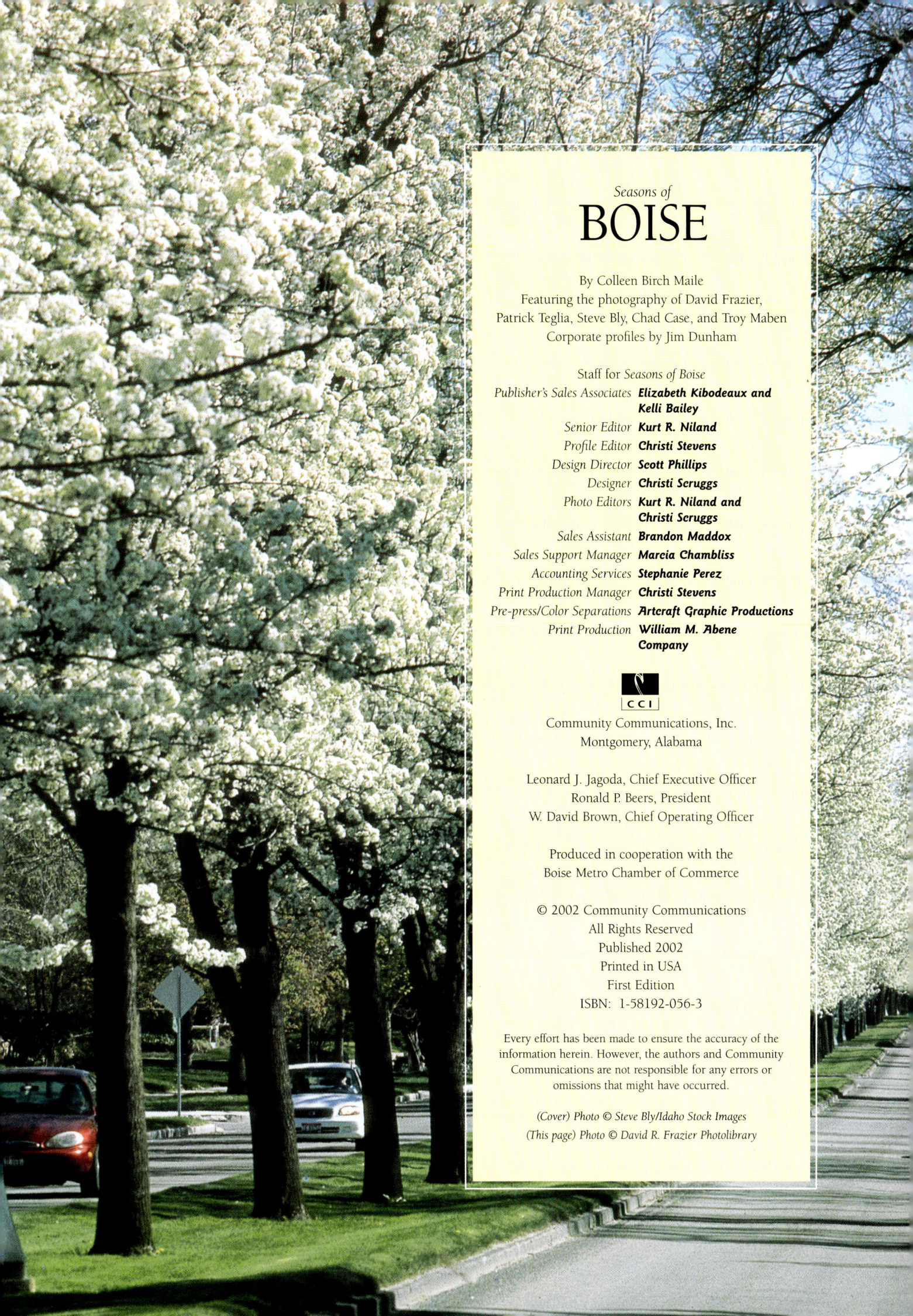

Seasons of
BOISE

By Colleen Birch Maile
Featuring the photography of David Frazier,
Patrick Teglia, Steve Bly, Chad Case, and Troy Maben
Corporate profiles by Jim Dunham

Staff for *Seasons of Boise*

Publisher's Sales Associates	**Elizabeth Kibodeaux and Kelli Bailey**
Senior Editor	**Kurt R. Niland**
Profile Editor	**Christi Stevens**
Design Director	**Scott Phillips**
Designer	**Christi Scruggs**
Photo Editors	**Kurt R. Niland and Christi Scruggs**
Sales Assistant	**Brandon Maddox**
Sales Support Manager	**Marcia Chambliss**
Accounting Services	**Stephanie Perez**
Print Production Manager	**Christi Stevens**
Pre-press/Color Separations	**Arteraft Graphic Productions**
Print Production	**William M. Abene Company**

cci

Community Communications, Inc.
Montgomery, Alabama

Leonard J. Jagoda, Chief Executive Officer
Ronald P. Beers, President
W. David Brown, Chief Operating Officer

Produced in cooperation with the
Boise Metro Chamber of Commerce

© 2002 Community Communications
All Rights Reserved
Published 2002
Printed in USA
First Edition
ISBN: 1-58192-056-3

Every effort has been made to ensure the accuracy of the
information herein. However, the authors and Community
Communications are not responsible for any errors or
omissions that might have occurred.

(Cover) Photo © Steve Bly/Idaho Stock Images
(This page) Photo © David R. Frazier Photolibrary

Contents

PREFACE, **8** FOREWORD, **10**

CHAPTER ONE: Introduction
Boise: Where People Make A Difference **12**

Save for a swath of green by the river, the area that is now Boise was once little more than a rough and ragged territory—a barren landscape punctuated with slap-dash structures and sagebrush. How the land came to be known as the "City of Trees," and how it has since transformed into the thriving, dynamic city it is today, is the fascinating story of pioneers and politicians, entrepreneurs and everyday people who have navigated Boise to success.

CHAPTER TWO: Spring
The Season of Optimism **34**

In Boise, springtime is more than an appointment with the vernal equinox. It is an attitude—light and vibrant as the kites that inspire an annual festival. Impetuous, too. Sometimes spring materializes on a February afternoon so balmy that crocuses sprout and school kids abandon coats and hats.

CHAPTER THREE: Summer
The Season of Opportunity **50**

If summer days seem brighter in Boise it's no illusion. During this season, purple mountains erupt against cornflower-colored skies. Sunset's pastels cast the arid foothills in shades of gold. Even city lawns seem greener than those elsewhere. Boise's high, dry climate allows summer's abundant light to shine pure, revealing an exceptionally vivid landscape.

CHAPTER FOUR: Autumn
The Season of Harvest **68**

When the foothills turn the color of dusty wheat, life gently downshifts in the Treasure Valley. The delightful commotion of summer wanes gradually. Outdoor entertainment and enterprises go on, albeit at a more relaxed pace. No one wants to squander the sunny afternoons and pleasant temperatures that often linger into November.

CHAPTER FIVE: Winter
A Season of Celebration **82**

For much of the winter season, steel-colored clouds hang low over the valley and the river churns in shades of indigo and gray. Snow rarely falls on Boise and almost never coats the ground. This is a settled time, when the land rests easy, and citizens find ample reason for glad tidings and good cheer.

ENTERPRISE INDEX, *162*   INDEX, *164*

CHAPTER SIX
Manufacturing, Distribution, High Technology & Communication *96*

Hewlett-Packard, 98 • DIRECTV Boise Customer Contact Center, 100
Building Materials Holding Corporation, 101 • Time Warner Telecom, 102

CHAPTER SEVEN
Business & Finance *104*

United Heritage, 106 • The Boise Metro Chamber of Commerce, 110
Wells Fargo, 112 • KeyBank, 113 • Great West Casualty Company, 114

CHAPTER EIGHT
The Professions *116*

Holland & Hart LLP, 118 • Atwood-Hinzman-Jones, 120 • CH2M Hill, 121
Leatham-Krohn-Van Ocker, Architects, 122
Hawley Troxell Ennis & Hawley LLP, 123 • habitec, 124

CHAPTER NINE
Real Estate, Development & Construction *126*

Steed Construction, 128 • Thornton Oliver Keller, 132
John L. Scott Real Estate, 134 • Petra, 136
F&C Corporation and Rocky Mountain Management & Development, LLC, 138
CM Company, Inc., 139

CHAPTER TEN
Health Care & Quality of Life *140*

Saint Alphonsus Regional Medical Center, 142 • Blue Cross of Idaho, 146
St. Luke's Regional Medical Center, 148 • Boise Heart Clinic, 150
Regence BlueShield of Idaho, 151

CHAPTER ELEVEN
The Marketplace, Hospitality & Tourism *152*

WestCoast ParkCenter Suites, 154 • AmeriSuites, 156
The Bon Marché, 158 • Meridian Ford, 160
Karen Louise Fashion Boutique, 161

Preface

Random chance brought my husband and me to this valley more than two decades ago. Choice kept us here. To most of our back-east family and friends, the decision to live our lives on what they termed "the outskirts of everywhere" was more than baffling. It was insane. But then they'd never been to Boise. They didn't know how the morning sun materializes above purple mountains majestic enough to inspire song. They hadn't seen twilight turn dusty foothills a dozen shades of lavender and gold. They couldn't comprehend a place where it was possible to hike before breakfast, fly-fish over the noon hour, and take the kids skiing after school—where winter merely flirted with the occasional snow flurry and summer's days seemed endless.

While its natural attributes remain enticing, the place we now call home differs vastly from the valley we first loved. In recent years, Boise has benefited from good fortune laced with irony. The city we initially encountered languished in the midst of a tortuous urban redevelopment. Whole downtown blocks were laid bare and a shopping spree required a plane ticket. With the 1990s, the dearth of construction ended and decades spent dreaming of what a city should be paid off. The result— a blossoming metropolis long on urban lifestyle and recreational opportunities.

This book attempts to capture the vibrancy of a place that is more than bricks and mortar, festivals and events, hills and streams. In all seasons, life in Boise is a testimony to people who, with resilience and drive, created an enterprising community in a high, dry, and beautiful place. If dedications are in order, this book is for friendly, hard-working Idahoans, eager to share the good life—people who welcomed newcomers like me. It's also for my fellow transplants, the legions of citizens who are here by choice, not circumstance.

Along those lines, particular kudos are appropriate. I'd like to commend the Boise Metro Chamber of Commerce for making this project possible and especially that organization's Mikel Ward and Amy Doyle for their encouragement, support, and keen insight into the finer points of life in the City of Trees. I'd also like to thank my husband, Tom Maile, for pitching the tent at the corner of Horseshoe Bend and Beacon Light Roads, so many years ago.

Colleen Birch Maile
August 12, 2002

Photo © Steve Bly/Idaho Stock Images

Foreword

Seasons of Boise captures the beauty and essence of the Boise metro area as it is today and gives the reader significant insight into what drives our area economy.

Boise and the surrounding area play a key role in the region. The area's future remains bright. We are confident that we will continue to see sustained, significant growth. The favorable business climate, solid economic base, and well-educated workforce continue to attract business and industry. The Boise area offers a high quality of life, through cultural activities, quality entertainment, sports and recreation, access to first-class health care, and educational opportunities. This high quality of life continues to draw workers and families from all over the United States and even the world.

This book provides an overview of the Boise metro area and the business climate, and offers a peek at the many arts, cultural, recreational, athletic, and educational opportunities that abound here. The reader will find that Boise offers much more than a great place to work, it is a wonderful place in which to live and raise a family. Readers will be introduced to many of the companies, organizations, products, entrepreneurs, and other leaders that have all helped the Boise area become the regional center for industry that it is today.

The Boise Metro Chamber of Commerce hopes this book will provide the reader with a sense of what makes this a unique place to call home. Ours is truly a special community—we hope that as the reader takes this visual tour, they will come to appreciate its uniqueness as well.

Nancy Vannorsdel
President & CEO
Boise Metro Chamber of Commerce

North End streets and city parks are a riot of colorful leaves during Boise's autumn. *Photo © David R. Frazier Photolibrary*

Part One

1

INTRODUCTION

Boise: Where People Make a Difference

(Previous page) In the Treasure Valley, citizens enjoy the best of divergent worlds. While snowplows seldom get a workout in the City of Trees, Boise's situation at the foothills of the Rockies offers ready access to deep-powder and all the fun it brings. *Photo © Steve Bly/Idaho Stock Images*

Idaho's state capitol was designed by J.E. Tourtellotte and Company in the neoclassical style patterned after the United States Capitol. Construction of the center section began in 1905 and was completed seven years later. It took until 1920 to complete the east and west wings. *Photo © Steve Bly/Idaho Stock Images*

(Above) Each year, from January through March, the state capitol hums with legislative activity. Spectators fill the fourth floor gallery to watch lawmakers work. Here, members of the House of Representatives convene. *Photo © David R. Frazier Photolibrary*

(Opposite) The fountain at Boise City Hall adds a splash of color and coolness to the downtown area. *Photo © Steve Bly/Idaho Stock Images*

Boise's nickname, "the City of Trees," might seem incongruous to visitors expecting a community carved from deep woods. The largest metropolis between Salt Lake City and Portland is a high-desert oasis creeping across flat-topped mesas to hug the sunset side of the Rockies. Tradition has it that the moniker came from the first Europeans to encounter this place. Sometime prior to 1836, when maps began denoting the "Boise River," French trappers rode in from the high desert, sighted vegetation along the waterway's banks and gleefully exclaimed, "les bois, les bois," (the woody place)!

To this day, arid foothills around Idaho's capital remain a shifting palette of subtle hues, from dusky green in spring to muted autumn gold. However, Boise City, the centerpiece of the Treasure Valley, lives up to its verdant title, thanks to determined and inventive citizens. The transformation was no simple task. When named state capital in 1864, Boise was a rough and ragged Army post. Its meager retail center catered to miners, Civil War renegades, and travelers heading east on the Oregon Trail. Many of these sojourners had passed through years earlier, bound for a more hospitable place. Idaho's gold fields lured them back to a hard and barren countryside punctuated with slap-dash structures, sagebrush, and a wide patch of green by the river. There, Boise City pioneer, Thomas Jefferson Davis, dug trenches to water an orchard. His seven thousand fruit trees altered the landscape forever.

By the start of the twentieth century, other farmers, aided by the federal government's fledgling Bureau of Reclamation, created a system of reservoirs, canals, and ditches to route melted snow from the mountains. Crops grew abundantly. So did an entrepreneurial spirit.

Builders and engineers based in the City of Trees helped revolutionize the West with roads, dams, and bridges. Among the most notable were Harry Morrison and Morris Hans Knudsen. By the 1930s, their Morrison-Knudsen Company was an international construction dynamo. During the same decade, Boise grocer, Joe Albertson, opened a store that spawned what is now one of

(Above) In 2002, Ada County's judicial system consolidated its services at this courthouse, located on 14.5 acres of prime downtown space. The innovative facility is part of a multi-use development that will include retail shops, eateries, and even some residential units—all within an easy stroll of the county's seat of justice. *Photo © Steve Bly/Idaho Stock Images*

(Right) No matter what season, dedication to community and country is evident throughout Boise, a city that truly embodies the American spirit. *Photo © Troy Maben/Idaho Stock Images*

America's largest food and drug retailers, and Jack Simplot, the man who gave McDonald's French fries and Idaho much more, established potato-packing plants throughout Southern Idaho. In the process, he honed an integrated business plan that made him Idaho's first billionaire. Today his Simplot Agribusiness feeds the world.

Boiseans have long been players in a global marketplace. Boise Cascade, Extended Systems, and homegrown titan, Micron Technology, all maintain headquarters in the City of Trees. Other major corporations, such as Hewlett-Packard, have a strong Boise presence. During the 1990s, record numbers of businesses, large and small, relocated to this valley from throughout the nation. So did tens of thousands of individuals. There are many drawing cards. Boise enjoys a moderate four-season climate, an annual average of 234 sunny days, exceptional recreational opportunities, and a quality lifestyle. Above all, it is home to people determined to make a positive difference in their world.

The citizens of Boise are accustomed to charting their own course, by overcoming obstacles and creating opportunities. The community they have built is more than a center of regional commerce, higher education, health care, and transportation. It is more than the seat of government, more than an outstanding convention and meeting destination, more than the gateway to incomparable recreational opportunities presented by nearby mountains, deserts, waterways, and the largest expanse of wilderness in the contiguous United States. Boise is a place people love to call home. Community pride is evident in flower-laden downtown streets, carefully landscaped public buildings, a wealth of parks, preserves, artistic venues, and tidy neighborhoods.

Saint Alphonsus Hospital became Boise's first healthcare facility in 1894. Six years later, it was joined by St. Luke's Regional Medical Center, which operates the Air St. Luke's EMS helicopter service (left). In 1972, Saint Al's moved from its downtown location to better serve a sprawling population. Through the years St.Luke's also expanded, enlarging its central location and building other outlying facilities. Together, these award-winning medical centers provide Boise and surrounding communities with state-of-the-art health care. *(Left) Photo © St. Luke's Regional Medical Center; (Below) Photo © David R. Frazier Photolibrary*

Scenic vistas, local color, and sidewalk eateries all enhance the casual ambience of downtown, and all are a vital part of the Boise experience. *(Above) Photo © Steve Bly/Idaho Stock Images; (Top opposite) Photo © Troy Mabel/Idaho Stock Images; (Bottom opposite) Photo © Chad Case/Idaho Stock Images*

National media laud this city's family-oriented lifestyle, modest crime rate, and business opportunities—even the golf and mountain biking. Locals don't need to read the news to know they've got a good thing. You can see it in their smiles.

Throughout the year, the people of Boise find ample cause to rejoice. They delight in their surroundings, celebrating their river, a foothills "fun run," and the nearby ski resort with equal gusto. They revel in the performing and visual arts and salute the intriguing mix of cultures that shape Idaho's heritage. They find countless ways to raise funds for causes that are as diverse as the Boise landscape.

With each change of seasons comes a fresh bounty of diversions. Golf, soccer, and horse racing in spring; camping, hiking, whitewater rafting in summer; football and hunting in fall; skiing and snowmobiling in winter—the list goes on and on. Yet, there is more to this place than fun and festivities. The essence of Boise's good life is in its homes and schools, businesses and neighborhoods, community centers and places of worship. Wherever people come together to solve problems, make the most of their potential, and craft a better future, Boise's resourceful legacy endures. ■

"Steed Construction first opened for business in the Bay Area of California. My partner Scott Raymes moved to Boise in 1983 to provide a better life for his family. He called me and wanted to know if we would be interested in opening a second office here in Boise. When I saw that the area was ripe for business and able to provide my family with a better lifestyle than in the Bay Area, we moved the family and the business here. Boise is the perfect city for business development and raising a family."

Randy Steed
President and Founder
Steed Construction, Inc.

The Boise River Greenbelt, which extends from one end of the county to the other, provides a haven for recreation and relaxation in the heart of the city. Just outside the city, ample year-round opportunities exist for outdoor enthusiasts. *Photos © Troy Maben/Idaho Stock Images*

The Idaho Anne Frank Human Rights Memorial is situated in the heart of Boise's cultural district at the intersection of the Boise Greenbelt and 8th Street. According to the memorial's organizers, it "is designed to appeal to people's highest human and spiritual instincts. It will remind us of the terrible costs of failing to act when action is required. It will speak to the very finest within all people, recalling a child who, though imprisoned in an attic by evil in the guise of patriotism, chose to trust in the human spirit." *(Left) Photo © David R. Frazier Photolibrary; (Below) Photo © Chad Case/Idaho Stock Images*

Boise's population increased as the local economy soared in the 1990s. The building industry responded by creating a wide variety of residential options. From townhouses to elaborate homes surrounded by acres of landscaping, the Treasure Valley housing market offers something for everyone. The city works hard to meet an ever-increasing demand for neighborhood parks and recreational opportunities. *(Above) Photo © Steve Bly/Idaho Stock Images; (Right) Photo © Patrick Teglia; (Opposite) Photo © David R. Frazier Photolibrary*

(Opposite) The Boise area is served by Idaho's two largest public school districts. Whether a child is enrolled in one of Boise's public or private schools, he or she will enjoy the region's highest standards of academic excellence. *(Top opposite) Photo © David R. Frazier Photolibrary; (Bottom opposite) Photo © Troy Maben/Idaho Stock Images*

(Above and left) Boise is home to Idaho's largest state institution of higher learning—Boise State University. The sprawling BSU campus plays host to a variety of cultural and athletic venues. A number of other nationally acclaimed private institutions are located in the Treasure Valley, including Northwest Nazarene University in Nampa and Caldwell's Albertson College of Idaho. *Photos © Steve Bly/Idaho Stock Images*

Boise is connected to the world by a solid transportation system. Whether by interstate or aircraft, people and goods come and go with ease, and major businesses, such as the valley's largest employer Micron Technology, engage in global commerce. The Boise Airport not only provides a critical link for passengers arriving in or departing from the city, it serves as the primary commercial service airport in southwestern Idaho, with a service area actually extending well into eastern Oregon. *(Above and top opposite) Photo © Steve Bly/Idaho Stock Images; (Bottom opposite) Photo © Troy Maben/Idaho Stock Images*

(Following pages) The many faces of business in Boise represent the world's finest, be it potatoes, computer technology, or financial services. *(Left) Photo © David R. Frazier Photolibrary; (Right) Photo © Steve Bly/Idaho Stock Images*

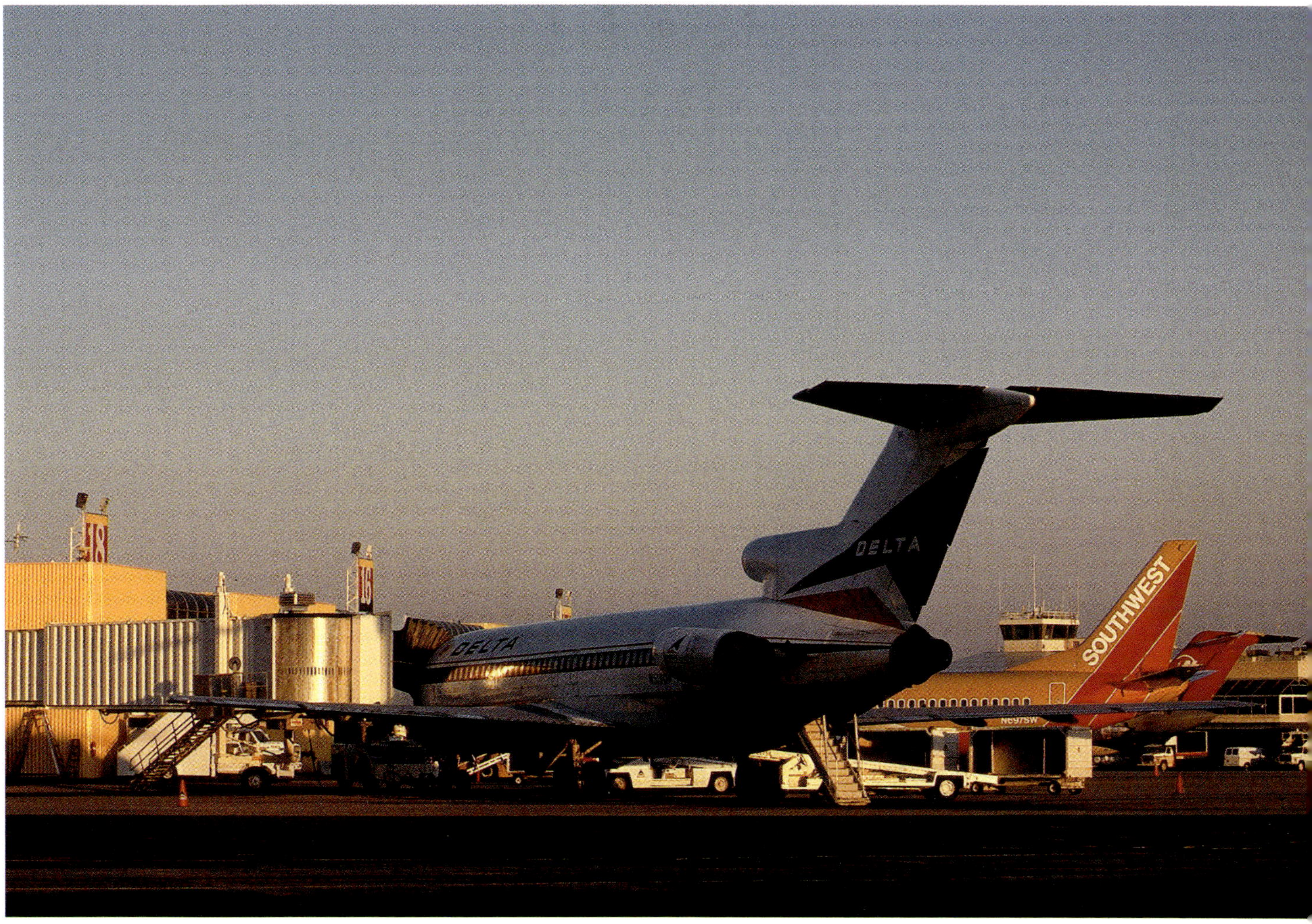
18
16
DELTA
DELTA
SOUTHWEST

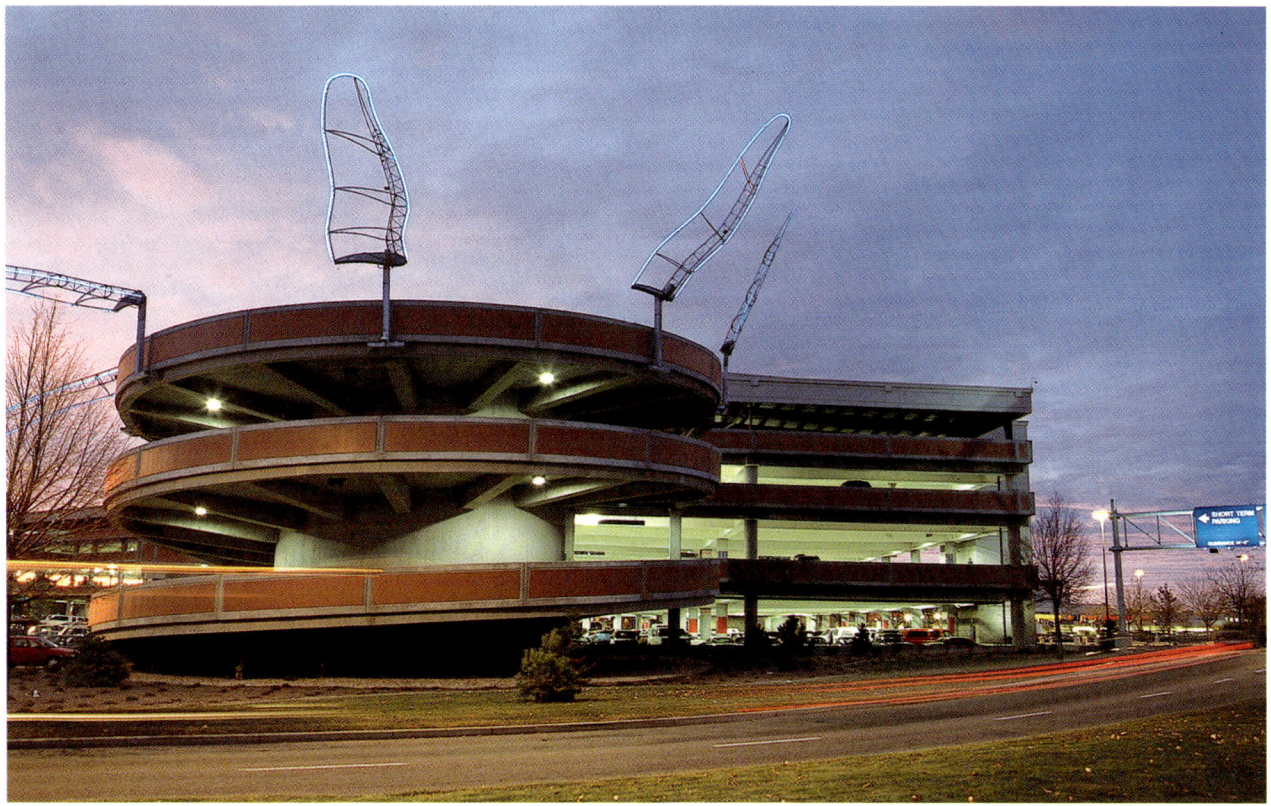

Seasons of Boise

Cultural opportunities abound in the City of Trees—the offerings of the Idaho Dance Theater, the Idaho Shakespeare Festival's repertory theater, music al fresco in the Gene Harris Bandshell, and films and other performances presented in the historic Egyptian Theater are all part of the fun.
(Top opposite) Photo courtesy of Idaho Dance Theater; (Bottom opposite) Photo © Troy Maben/Idaho Stock Images; (Above) Photo courtesy of the Idaho Shakespeare Festival; (Left) Photo © Steve Bly/Idaho Stock Images

2

SPRING

The Season of Optimism

Boiseans enjoy authentic Mexican food, watch folkloric dancers, and listen to Mariachi bands at the annual Cinco de Mayo celebration sponsored by Boise State University's Organizacion de Estudiantes Latino-Americanos. *Photo © David R. Frazier Photolibrary*

(Opposite) Despite a blatant disregard for schedules, Boise's springtime fulfills every seasonal stereotype. March blusters into the City of Trees, full of breezy hope and the scent of rising sap. *Photo © Troy Maben/Idaho Stock Images*

(Above) Each spring, vibrant irises beautify area landscapes and draw throngs to commercial gardens where "designer" hybrids in every imaginable hue are offered for sale. *Photo © Patrick Teglia*

In Boise, springtime is more than an appointment with the vernal equinox. It is an attitude—light and vibrant as the kites that inspire an annual festival. Impetuous, too. Sometimes spring materializes on a February afternoon so balmy that crocuses sprout and school kids abandon coats and hats. Brilliant March skies can entice Bogus Basin skiers to wear shorts, while in the valley, short-sleeved golfers tee-up. However, premature sunshine and songbirds don't fool old-timers. They won't declare winter's end until the snow recedes from Shaefer's Butte to the city's east and the Boise River swells with mountain runoff. Even then, this fickle season sometimes dusts tulips and daffodils with April snow.

Despite a blatant disregard for schedules, Boise's springtime fulfills every seasonal stereotype. March blusters in, full of breezy hope and the scent of rising sap. The woods along the river, comprised of native vegetation, inspire a sense of optimism. In the snarls of budding cottonwoods and willows, anglers cast from the riverbank. These waters shelter trout—rainbows and browns, native and stocked. Fishing holes are as ample as they are accessible. A paved 25-mile Greenbelt skirts the banks for the entire breadth of the county. Meandering within a mile of the State Capitol, it offers a perfect antidote for spring fever. Here, Boise workers can encounter nature over the noon hour. Bicyclists and birdwatchers, rollerbladers and runners, as well as folks engaged in a leisurely stroll easily shrug off winter beside this rushing stream.

On the edge of downtown, the river and its pathway bisect Boise State University's campus. The school is home to the elegant Morrison Center for the Performing Arts and the BSU Pavilion—a venue for road shows, sporting events, and more. Adjacent to the university, in Julia Davis Park, the river provides a fitting backdrop for spring concerts and a wealth of other activity in the band shell. In this, the grand dame of Boise's exceptional park system, children scramble across playgrounds, ramble through Zoo Boise, and learn that science is hands-on fun at the Discovery Center. Equally provocative cultural repositories—The Boise Art Museum, the Idaho

On high school fields, city streets, and community bike paths, Boiseans love to engage in serious springtime fun. *Photo © Troy Maben/Idaho Stock Images*

"Our firm's approach to business has always been centered upon a promise to represent properties that are well located, well designed, and well built. This approach has proven successful because Boise is going to continue to grow with a stable supply of local and regional companies. We believe Boise will become a city which will service an emerging regional market. As the city grows, we'll work to continue delivering high quality personal service."

Peter Oliver
Partner
Thornton Oliver Keller

Historical Museum, and the Idaho Black History Museum—lure Julia Davis visitors with attractions unique to the city and its region.

Just to the west, the Greenbelt winds beneath Capitol Boulevard to link office complexes and restaurants with the 153-acre Ann Morrison Park, site of playing fields, tennis courts, and picnic spots. Like other green places throughout the valley, this park draws kids who welcome spring with the crack of Little League bats and the frenzy of soccer matches. Adults play those games and more. In preparation for an active Idaho summer, thousands of Boiseans huff along a rugged mountain path during the "Race to Robie Creek." This fundraiser for various social causes may be America's toughest thirteen-mile run. Its innovative send-offs and finish-line celebrations are equally legendary.

But then this is a place that knows how to make merry. In springtime, Boise's good mood spills across the valley. Along pedestrian-friendly 8th Street, in the North End's quaint Hyde Park and other neighborhoods around town, sidewalk eateries mark the season with unfurled umbrellas and a bounty of blossoms. The party atmosphere extends to organized festivities. Many of them center on

(Above) The most esteemed cycling race for women in the world is the HP Women's Challenge, which has consistently raised the bar for female athletes since 1984. According to its organizers, the HP Women's Challenge is in many ways like the Tour de France for male cyclists: "While the men tour the French countryside, the women tackle the HP Women's Challenge, pitting themselves against each other and the rugged terrain of Idaho." *Photo © Steve Bly/Idaho Stock Images*

(Left) Recreational mountain biking in Boise's foothills is a favorite pastime for residents and visitors alike. *Photo © Steve Bly/Idaho Stock Images*

song. In 1919, Boise launched the nation's first community-wide Music Week. The tradition endures as citizens young and old gather to produce seven-days' worth of free entertainment—everything from sing-alongs to operas to musicales.

Above all, Boise has long-held an affinity for jazz. Each April, the Gene Harris Jazz Festival is the hottest three-day ticket in town. Notable musicians, including those of international renown, fill Boise clubs, jam on the Pavilion's grand stage, and fund scholarships for Boise State University students. It's all in tribute to Harris, the late, great pianist who made his home in the "City of Trees."

Throughout the year Boiseans seize every opportunity to honor the community's diverse and unique heritage. In spring, Saint Patrick's Day parties, Easter egg hunts, and Cinco de Mayo fiestas are embraced by people of varied ancestries. Other, more personal observances also mark the season. Members of Boise's Jewish community, stewards of the oldest continually operating synagogue in the West, remember the deliverance from Egypt at Passover. Christians observe Easter sunrise with an array of services including those in Boise's fresh, green foothills.

The robust scenery testifies that this is the time of renewal. Each lengthening day holds promise of a joyful and active summer. ■

(Above) Boise serves as the gateway to the largest expanse of wilderness in the lower 48 states. However, those who prefer to drive to their campsite can find plenty of places to pitch a tent on readily accessible National Forest and Bureau of Land Management property.
Photo © David R. Frazier Photolibrary

(Opposite top) An hour to Boise's east, Bruneau Sand Dunes State Park is another ideal spring destination. It includes the largest single-structured sand dune in North America. As shadows shift throughout the day, photographers seek to capture the environment's beauty. At night it is a haven for stargazers. *Photo © Steve Bly/Idaho Stock Images*

(Opposite bottom) South of the Bruneau Sand Dunes, the stunning Bruneau Canyon splits the desert flats. Bighorn sheep and antelope thrive in the area, and the elaborate drawings of the Paiute Indians, who originally discovered the canyon centuries ago, can be seen on rock slabs throughout the desert. *Photo © Josh Roper/Idaho Stock Images*

Julia Davis Park is a cultural focal point for the Boise region. It became Boise's first city recreation area in 1907 when pioneer Tom Davis donated 43 acres of orchard land near the river for public use. The park is dedicated to Davis' wife, who died after aiding a traveler sick with typhoid fever. The Boise Art Museum, a facility that has received national recognition for leadership, innovation, and excellence in the visual arts, as well as the Idaho State Historical Museum, the Black History Museum, the Discovery Center, and Zoo Boise are all located within the park, which now encompasses almost 90 acres in the heart of the city.
(Opposite) Photo © Patrick Teglia; (Above) Photo © Troy Maben/Idaho Stock Images; (Left) Photo © Steve Bly/Idaho Stock Images

(Above) The Boise Tour Train is a familiar downtown site. Its passengers enjoy highly informative encounters with significant places throughout the capital city. *Photo © Patrick Teglia*

(Right) As a teenager, Kentucky Derby-winning jockey Gary Stevens first rode to victory at Boise's Les Bois Park track. Beginning each May, horseracing fans enjoy a full season of live action competition. Simulcast events make it possible for locals to continue to bet on Stevens' mounts and other national contenders. *Photo © Patrick Teglia*

(Opposite) Tulips, among the first harbingers of spring, can appear in Boise as early as February. *Photo © Patrick Teglia*

(Opposite) Owned and maintained by the City of Boise, the Boise Depot is a popular venue in which to host special events. *Photo © Patrick Teglia*

(Above left) Boise's Music Week celebration presents an array of free performances showcasing local talent. *Photo © David R. Frazier Photolibrary*

(Above right) Boise's long-held affinity for jazz culminates each April with the Gene Harris Jazz Festival. Notable musicians, including those of international renown, fill Boise clubs, jam on the Pavilion's grand stage, and fund scholarships for Boise State University students, all in tribute to Harris, the late, great pianist who made his home in the "City of Trees." *Photo © Chad Case/Idaho Stock Images*

(Left) Trees blossom on the grounds of a local place of worship, introducing a season of renewal and rebirth. *Photo © Chad Case/Idaho Stock Images*

(Opposite) In preparation for an active Idaho summer, thousands of Boiseans huff along a rugged mountain path during the "Race to Robie Creek." This fundraiser for various social causes may be America's toughest thirteen-mile run. *Photo © Chad Case/Idaho Stock Photography*

(Above) The local chapter of the Susan G. Komen Breast Cancer Foundation sponsors the annual Race for the Cure in Boise each May. The race not only raises vital funds for breast cancer research but ties the community together in the spirit of philanthropy and hope.
Photo © Chad Case/Idaho Stock Photography

3

SUMMER

The Season of Opportunity

River rafting is an Idaho rite of summer. These paddlers enjoy a whitewater thrill on the mighty Payette just north of Boise. *Photo © David R. Frazier Photolibrary*

(Opposite) Summer evenings find the city's plazas and streets buzzing with activity. From live entertainment on the weekend to Boise's signature Alive After Five celebration at the Grove, to the bustling bistros, restaurants, and coffee shops, Boise entertains. *Photo © Steve Bly/Idaho Stock Images*

(Above) Children take a cool break in the fountain adjacent to the Boise Centre on the Grove. *Photo © David R. Frazier Photolibrary*

If summer days seem brighter in Boise, it's no illusion. During this season, purple mountains erupt against cornflower-colored skies. Sunset's pastels cast the arid foothills in shades of gold. Even city lawns seem greener than those elsewhere. The reason? Boise's high, dry climate allows summer's abundant light to shine pure, revealing an exceptionally vivid landscape.

It's also true that these lovely days linger. Compared to most of America, Boise benefits from nearly an extra hour of evening sun. Modern citizens can thank nineteenth-century politicians for this "phenomenon." In 1897, Boise's Council voted to align city clocks with those of the Mountain Time Zone and eastern Idaho, despite the fact that the Pacific Time Zone lies to the north, south, and west. The result of that decision, intensified by Daylight Savings Time, means that most summer sunsets occur after nine o'clock at night. It's a grand quirk. But, even with this sunny advantage, there are never enough hours in a day to pursue all that Boise offers.

Late into each evening, the valley whirs with activity. Golfers tee up. Softball teams gather for friendly competition. Tennis players crowd the area's ample courts. The aroma of backyard barbecue fills the air. Home-gardeners tend flowers and vegetable beds. Children splash at community pools.

Downtown radiates exuberance—especially on Wednesdays. A mid-week celebration, Alive After Five, has been rocking the Grove plaza for more than a decade. The best local bands make music. Area restaurants take turns serving food and drink. Kids frolic in the fountain. Dancers revel in the sunshine. Everybody smiles.

Culturally delicious events crowd summer's entire calendar. The Greek Festival at Saints Constantine and Helen's Church offers enormous quantities of baklava, dolmades, and other Mediterranean delectables. Boiseans nosh Kosher during Temple Ahaveth Beth Israel's Deli Days. Soul food is in order Juneteenth, when the African-American community commemorates the 1865 emancipation from slavery. Annually, Boise Basques honor their patron at the Festival of

A lofty wizard floats above downtown streets during the Boise River Festival's annual River Giants Parade. Volunteers, who are among the more than 4,000 Boiseans donating time and resources to the city's signature event, guide him. *Photo © David Spaulding/David R. Frazier Photolibrary*

San Inazio. Chorizos and other Old World dishes accompanied by traditional music, dancing, and games are highlights. Every five years, Jai Aldi, a gathering of Basques from throughout the nation and around the world, amplifies the festivities.

Boise's neighboring communities also honor distinct summer traditions. Canyon County retains its western attitude with Caldwell's Night Rodeo and Nampa's Snake River Stampede—both premiere cowboy events. Emmett has its Cherry Festival. Meridian does Dairy Days. Eagle cooks up the World's Largest Rocky Mountain Oyster Feed.

The grandest celebration of all is Boise's own award-winning River Festival. This citywide extravaganza features a mind-boggling agenda. One of the nation's finest balloon rallies launches the event. Throughout each day, city parks bustle with continuous entertainment and exhibits. During The River Giants Parade, enormous helium-inflated characters hover above city streets. The pageantry rivals Macy's Thanksgiving spectacle. After dark, things really get glowing. Hot-air balloons illuminate to the beat of music. A Night Lite parade dazzles downtown. The city's largest fireworks display, visible for miles, concludes each annual tribute to the river.

Despite all the fun, Boiseans don't need a special event to salute their namesake waterway—especially in summer. Floating the relatively gentle stretch of river between Barber Dam and Ann Morrison Park is a favorite way to spend a lazy afternoon. A series of thrilling, albeit small, rapids punctuate an easy journey. Those seeking the adrenaline-rush of rugged whitewater must look beyond this stream.

Some Boise customs link its people to a larger heritage. On Independence Day, citizens unfurl flags and march in parades. At season's end, they congregate at the Western Idaho Fair to delight in carnival rides, enjoy food and entertainment, and admire local enterprise in the form of 4-H projects, handicrafts, produce, and more. *Photos © Chad Case/Idaho Stock Images*

"For over a century, Saint Alphonsus has pioneered advancements to improve the health of our communities, in the spirit of a faith-based mission. We gain strength from the past but are focused on the future, encompassing innovation and technology within a healing environment. By recognizing the diverse and growing needs of the region's population, Saint Alphonsus is poised to deliver the highest caliber medical care, wellness, and prevention services well into the 21st century."

Sandra Bruce
President and CEO
Saint Alphonsus Regional Medical Center

They do not need to look far, however. The mighty Payette River rushes from the mountains north of Boise. A favorite launching spot for rafters and kayakers is just an hour away near Garden Valley. Other fun-filled mountain communities—McCall, Cascade, Idaho City, Stanley, and Sun Valley—are within easy scenic drives. All sit amid pristine mountain scenery, exceptional fishing streams, and ample backcountry opportunities.

Closer to home, Boise's foothills offer wide-open pleasure just minutes from town. Hikers, joggers, mountain bikers, equestrians and those inclined to zoom off-road in four-wheel-drive trucks and ATV's all find room to move along these gentle slopes. Just ten miles east of the city at Lucky Peak State Park, boaters and other water sports enthusiasts pursue their passions. Throughout the area, man-made lakes, ponds, and reservoirs, including the fourteen-square-mile Lake Lowell, offer ample opportunities for sailboats, windsurfers, and motorcraft. On these waters, anglers fish for trout, bass, crappies, perch and more.

Boiseans take advantage of the optimum climate with an array of al fresco entertainment. They sample the valley's bounty at farmers markets and wager on horses at Les Bois Park. Baseball fans cheer

the Hawks Class-A team. Racing buffs trek to Meridian and Emmett to watch stock cars and dragsters. Crowds line downtown sidewalks for a glimpse of the toughest race in women's cycling, the HP Women's Challenge. Hundreds turn out to listen to weekend jazz at a winery. Thousands attend big-name concerts at outdoor venues like the Idaho Center. Picnic-packing theater lovers flock to the Idaho Shakespeare Festival's riverside amphitheater, where the works of the Bard and other classical playwrights unfold beneath the stars.

Some Boise customs link its people to a larger heritage. On Independence Day, citizens unfurl flags and march in parades. At season's end they congregate at the Western Idaho Fair to delight in carnival rides, enjoy food and entertainment and admire local enterprise in the form of 4-H projects, handicrafts, produce and more. Day-by-day they salute the subtle rewards of freedom. All year through, life in this valley presents opportunities as sparkling and timeless as a Boise summer.

(Right) Boise may sport a dynamic, modern face, but not at the expense of its Western heritage. An affinity for horses and wide, open spaces are part of the area's undying cowboy culture. *Photo © David R. Frazier Photolibrary*

(Below) For the better part of a century, the nation's top cowboys have competed at the Snake River Stampede in Boise. The weeklong event remains a summer tradition in the Treasure Valley. Novelty acts, such as Roman Riding expert Blake Goode, add an extra measure of entertainment to the lineup. *Photo © Patrick Teglia*

(Left) Established in 1978 by the Symms Fruit Ranch, Inc., Ste. Chapelle Winery produces 130,000 cases of wine annually. These are distributed throughout the United States, Canada, Europe, and Taiwan. Carrying on Boise's jazz traditions, the winery hosts Jazz at the Winery, a summer event held on Sundays from mid June through late July. *Photo © Mark Lisk/Idaho Stock Images*

(Below) The Rose Garden in Julia Davis Park teems with some two hundred varieties of roses, making it a popular local setting for summer weddings and other special events. *Photo © Steve Bly/Idaho Stock Images*

(Opposite) Outdoor enthusiasts benefit from Boise's mild, dry climate. This golfer tees up at Eagle Hills public course, one of more than 20 golf courses and driving ranges in the valley. *Photo © Patrick Teglia*

(Above) Boaters moor their crafts at Spring Shores Marina at Lucky Peak Reservoir. *Photo © David R. Frazier Photolibrary*

(Left) Soccer players from throughout the region benefit from summer training camps and spring and autumn matches and tournaments held at the Simplot Sports Complex—among the West's finest soccer facilities. *Photo © David R. Frazier Photolibrary*

Weekly summer events in Boise include the bustling Farmers Market, held in the open air on 8th and Main Streets. Vendors from throughout the Boise region sell locally grown produce, fresh flowers, baked goods, and more at the market, creating a splash of summertime color and activity on the streets of downtown Boise. *(Above) Photo © Troy Maben/Idaho Stock Images; (Right) Photo © Steve Bly/Idaho Stock Images*

(Opposite) Silver City, the queen of Idaho ghost towns, is a bit of an anomaly. Once a thriving mining center and the Owyhee County seat from 1867 until 1935, it is now "inhabited" by a handful of summer residents who preserve the remaining properties in their original state. The Masonic Lodge, shown here, was once a bustling social center. Wildflowers dot the barren countryside around the historic settlement. *Photos © Patrick Teglia*

(Opposite) A swim in the community pool and a cool, refreshing float down the Boise River offer respite during a long, lazy summer day. *(Above) Photo © Troy Maben/Idaho Stock Images; (Below) Photo © David R. Frazier Photolibrary*

(Above) The Boise Hawks baseball team, an affiliate of the Chicago Cubs, plays Class A ball in the Northwest League. Fans root for the home team at Memorial Stadium adjacent to the Western Idaho Fairgrounds and Les Bois Race Track. *Photo © David R. Frazier Photolibrary*

Throughout the year, Boise's Basque Museum and Basque Block honor the unique cultural heritage of the people of the Pyrenees and their contributions to Idaho history. Each July, the San Inazio Festival celebrates the feast of Saint Ignatius of Loyola with special food and entertainment. The entire Boise community is invited to enjoy performances by the Bihotzetik Basque Choir and the internationally acclaimed Oinkari Basque Dancers. Competitions also showcase traditional feats of strength such as this "lumberjack" contest. *Photos © David R. Frazier Photolibrary*

(Opposite) A mile from the heart of Boise's downtown, Hyde Park became the city's first "suburban" development around the turn of the twentieth century. Today, the charming retail center remains a focal point for activity in the city's popular North End neighborhood. In close proximity to the foothills and several city parks it is a magnet for mountain bikers, a haven for children who delight in its candy store, and a gathering place for all who enjoy its ample dining options. *Photo © Steve Bly/Idaho Stock Images*

Seasons of Boise

(Above opposite) Southern cooking, deeply rooted in African, Caribbean, and European culinary traditions, is the highlight of Boise's annual Soul Food Extravaganza, held each summer in Julia Davis Park. African and African-American music and arts are also a feature of the festival, which seeks to "increase the awareness of African-American culture represented in the Treasure Valley Community through a shared, enlightening, entertaining, and educational experience, while supporting charitable causes in the community." *Photo © Steve Bly/Idaho Stock Images*

(Below opposite) Since 1953, nearby Weiser, Idaho has hosted fiddlers of all ages from around the world at its annual contest, the oldest and most prestigious of fiddling contests in the world. *Photo © Chad Case/Idaho Stock Images*

(Above) The first trappers to enter this valley were greeted by members of the Shoshone and Bannock tribes, a people the Europeans called "Snake Indians" because they used "snake sticks" to frighten travelers. Since 1989, Native Americans from throughout the United States, representing a variety of tribes and people, have gathered in the Treasure Valley at the International Montour Powwow. Events open to the public include dance and drum competitions and the selection of a Powwow Princess. *Photo © Patrick Teglia*

4
AUTUMN

The Season of Harvest

In autumn, the Boise River banks are lined with trees ablaze with leaves of orange and gold. *Photo © Steve Bly/Idaho Stock Images*

(Above) Kathryn Albertson Park is ablaze with fiery reds, oranges, and yellows once crisp autumn air sweeps into town. *Photo © Steve Bly/Idaho Stock Images*

(Opposite) Few of life's simple pleasures compare to a quiet glide down the Boise River, surrounded by the comforting sights and smells of autumn. *Photo © Steve Bly/Idaho Stock Images*

When the foothills turn the color of dusty wheat, life gently downshifts in the Treasure Valley. The delightful commotion of summer wanes gradually. Outdoor entertainment and enterprises go on, but at a more relaxed pace. No one wants to squander the sunny afternoons and pleasant temperatures that often linger into November.

Construction workers still labor to build a growing community. The city's rivers and ridges continue to beckon horsemen and hikers, mountain bikers and other open-air enthusiasts. Rock hounds scour the landscape for treasure. This is the Gem State, after all.

Cooler weather invites a trip to the desert. Early fall is the optimum time to visit Silver City southwest of Boise where a window to the past survives at the end of a washboard road. Once a thriving mining center, Silver City's glory days played out decades ago. Now, locals lovingly preserve dozens of the ghost town's structures including homes, a schoolhouse, and a hotel.

An hour to Boise's east, Bruneau Sand Dunes State Park is another ideal autumn destination. It includes the largest single-structured sand dune in North America. As shadows shift throughout the day, photographers seek to capture the environment's beauty. At night it is a haven for stargazers.

Twenty arid miles south of Boise, The Snake River Birds of Prey National Conservation Area is home to the largest number of nesting raptors in the nation. While spring is the best time to see babies, a wealth of recreational activities—camping, boating, hiking, and bird watching—make it an excellent autumn day-trip. Closer to Boise, the World Center for Birds of Prey, with its Velma Morrison Interpretive Center, offers a unique learning experience. All year long, it presents interactive exhibits, multi-media displays, and live birds including condors and eagles.

In the "City of Trees," the Greenbelt and other open spaces remain a constant source of convenient joy. Weekend traffic from Boise to McCall, Idaho City, and other mountain destinations diminishes in fall, except for caravans of hunters seeking elk and deer. School buses take to Treasure Valley roads. The area's colleges

(Above) Vibrant aspen and tamarack punctuate the evergreen mountain forests near Boise with spectacular autumn color. *Photo © David R. Frazier Photolibrary*

(Right and opposite) By boat, bike, or foot, there are a number of ways to enjoy Boise's fall foliage, be it in one of the city's parks or the outskirts of town. *(Right) Photo © Troy Maben/Idaho Stock Images; (Opposite) Photo © Steve Bly/Idaho Stock Images*

and universities welcome freshmen and returning students. Football fever spills from Boise State University to high schools and Youth Optimist fields throughout the valley. Soccer moms and dads spend weeknights in carpools and Saturdays on the sidelines.

An invisible sense of schedule and purpose permeates the city and countryside. At mall shops and schoolyards, playing fields and parks activities quicken and slow with regularity. Sunlight grows scarcer. Responsibilities resume. As always, Boiseans make the most of life's possibilities.

Autumn accommodates a slate of annual events. Fun Runs raise money for a variety of causes. The YMCA benefits as thousands of runners and walkers travel beside the Boise River from Barber Dam to Ann Morrison Park. Children under thirteen have their own YMCA race, The Harrison Classic which takes its name from the route along a historic Boise boulevard. The St. Luke's Idaho Women's Health and Fitness Education Celebration is the largest event of its kind in the nation. It draws thousands of women to its 5K Race and Women's Show.

Julia Davis Park becomes a festive marketplace during Art in the Park, one of the Northwest's most significant juried art shows. This traditional salute to creativity is presented by the Boise Art Museum

"I think that one of the greatest feathers in Boise's cap in recent years was the fact that this city put on the best Torch Run party in the United States during the 2002 Winter Olympics and were able to secure the Olympic cauldron in Boise. It amazes me that Boise was able to beat out the host city as far as enthusiasm for the event. United Heritage was honored and proud to serve as one of the major local advertisers of the Olympics."

Dennis Johnson
CEO
United Heritage

In Boise, autumn connotations of sport range from football field to field and stream. For thousands of Boiseans, many fall weekends are dedicated to exciting home games at Bronco Stadium cheering for the Broncos. On a much quieter note, bird hunters find ample opportunity to bag ducks and geese along Canyon County waterways such as Lake Lowell and the Snake River. *(Opposite) Photo © Kevin Syms/David Frazier Photolibrary; (Above and right) Photos © Steve Bly/Idaho Stock Images*

in early September. Later that month, Julia Davis visitors encounter Idaho's heritage, up close and personal. The Historical Museum "Comes to Life" as trappers, prospectors, homesteaders, and other personalities from the past demonstrate all-but-forgotten skills.

When frost signals a serious change of season, Boise trees put on a showy display. In adjacent Canyon County, chilly mornings make apples crisp and "U-Pick" signs line roadways. Compelled more by custom than need, city dwellers wander country lanes. They find the chance to roam orchards and sip fresh cider as enticing as the produce.

This is a season long on tradition. Boiseans of all ages ramble through pumpkin patches pursuing the perfect candidate for a jack-o-lantern. They get lost in corn mazes, scare themselves silly at haunted houses, and seek occasions to wear costumes. Not the least of these is the annual Boo at the Zoo fund-raiser for Zoo Boise.

Like so many generations before them, trick-or-treating children crunch through Boise's fallen leaves. Spooky décor is on display at

homes throughout the valley for much of October. Churches and community centers celebrate the season of harvest with festivals and concerts.

Increasingly, Boise's cultural pursuits move indoors. Opera Idaho launches its season at the Morrison Center for the Performing Arts. The Boise Philharmonic takes to that stage and also performs at Nampa's Civic Center. For more than fifty years, the Boise Little Theater has showcased local talent. Other homegrown performing troupes offer everything from original works at Boise Contemporary Theater to tried-and-true classics served up with dinner.

As the harvest moon grows large and the year grows old, Boiseans reflect on the benefits of a rich and varied lifestyle. There is much cause for Thanksgiving.

(Above) Although year-round schools are an option in some parts of the valley, the vast majority of students return to classrooms during autumn. Because warm weather often lingers into October, back-to-school wardrobes typically include shorts and t-shirts. *Photo © David R. Frazier Photolibrary*

(Right) Tree-lined streets help Boise live up to its nickname and add to the charm of the many well-established neighborhoods. *Photo © David R. Frazier Photolibrary*

(Opposite) During the Boise Art Museum's annual Art in the Park event, visual artists and craftspeople display their creations in Julia Davis Park while local performers take to the bandshell's stage. Throughout the long weekend, children such as those shown here explore their own artistic expressions. *Photo © David R. Frazier Photolibrary*

(Right) Boise Contemporary Theater presents high-quality theatrical works—especially plays exploring contemporary life—at the Fulton Street Theater in the heart of Boise's emerging entertainment district. The theater is housed in the former Frontier Wholesale Warehouse, which was built in 1935. Its 26,836 square feet provide reasonably priced space for a variety of arts groups. As the facility's resident company, Boise Contemporary Theater works to foster the training of theater students and also presents an annual season of first-class performances.
Photo courtesy of Boise Contemporary Theater

(Opposite and below) Finding the perfect candidate for a jack-o-lantern is always cause for youthful delight. Boise area children can select from pumpkin patches or neighborhood markets such as the one shown here.
(Opposite) Photo © David R. Frazier Photolibrary; (Below) Photo © Troy Maben/Idaho Stock Images

(Opposite) The valley, with its mild, arid climate, provides a hospitable winter range for cattle like the herd silhouetted against this expansive October sky. *(Top) Photo © David R. Frazier Photolibrary; (Bottom) Photo © Steve Bly/Idaho Stock Images*

(Left) Established in 1970, The Peregrine Fund works nationally and internationally to conserve birds of prey in their natural habitats. The Boise-based organization actively works to restore species in jeopardy, conserve habitats, educate students, train conservationists, provide factual information to the public, and accomplish good science for the benefit of all earth's inhabitants. The World Center for Birds of Prey and the Velma Morrison Interpretive Center serve as headquarters for the Peregrine Fund and are open to the public interested in its mission. *Photo © Steve Bly/Idaho Stock Images*

(Below) Although the Boise River Zone is one of Idaho's most popular big game areas, autumn expeditions to high country hunting grounds where snow is always a possibility are also a long-standing Boise tradition. *Photo © Steve Bly/Idaho Stock Images*

5

WINTER

*A Season
of
Celebration*

Just 16 miles from downtown Boise, Bogus Basin ski resort offers more than 2,000 acres of skiable terrain, including one of America's longest night runs. There's nothing "bogus" about the alpine experience on this mountain. The name dates to Idaho's mining heyday when a group of ne'er do wells led by one Captain Tom Morgan mined pyrite ("fool's gold") from the site and passed it off as the real thing. Today, the mountain offers a wealth of fun and amenities including sleigh rides, mid-mountain lodging and runs sure to please all ages and abilities of skiers and snowboarders. *Photo © David R. Frazier Photolibrary*

The snow level often reaches down to coat the Boise foothills but rarely covers the valley. Area children enjoy tubing and tobogganing in the higher elevations of Garden Valley and McCall and wait for those special occasions when deep drifts make the hills of Boise's Camel Back Park slick enough for sleds. *Photo © David R. Frazier Photolibrary; (Opposite) Photo © Chad Case/Idaho Stock Images*

For much of the winter season, steel-colored clouds hang low over the valley and the river churns in shades of indigo and gray. Snow rarely falls on Boise and almost never coats the ground. This is a settled time, when the land rests easy and citizens find ample reason for glad tidings and good cheer.

The holiday spirit arrives early. Fund-raising bazaars and Christmas craft sales, such as the Boise Art Museum's Beaux Arts extravaganza, begin in November. That's also when Santa Claus shows up. He graces downtown Boise's Holiday Parade, enlivens Meridian's Festival of Wreaths, and draws crowds to the Towne Square Mall.

During Thanksgiving weekend, the Festival of Trees, sponsored by Saint Alphonsus Regional Medical Center, transforms the Boise Center on the Grove into a creative wonderland. Lavishly decorated trees, elaborate gingerbread structures, ample entertainment, a gala and an auction help raise money for special "Saint Al's" projects. At the valley's other major health care facility, St. Luke's Regional Medical Center, volunteers busily fill orders for Christmas cards created by local artists. These images, suitable for framing, do more than help support the hospital. Their unique reflections of Idaho life are a long-standing part of Boise's holiday scene.

Traditional entertainment is further cause for seasonal rejoicing. Area dance students join Ballet Idaho company members for a delightful interpretation of *The Nutcracker*. The Boise Master Chorale performs Handel's *Messiah*. Churches produce living Nativity Scenes. Schools celebrate winter's pageantry. Local theater groups stage at least one rendition of *A Christmas Carol*. City streets and neighborhoods throughout the valley glow with festive displays. Communities come together to light trees and candles, fill the night sky with the sound of ancient carols, and give gifts to those in need.

Boise is a city with a strong social conscience. Food drives are as much a part of the holiday season as trees and tinsel. Boy Scouts and other volunteers typically gather more than a hundred thousand pounds of groceries for the local Food Bank. Business, civic, and religious groups reach out to the elderly, homeless, and working poor. Residents of Community House, the Boise Rescue Mission, and the

City of Light Women and Children's Shelter benefit from the kindness of their neighbors during the holidays and throughout the year.

A communal commitment to good deeds also is reflected in the Humanitarian Bowl football game. Since 1997, Boise has closed out the year with a clash between Western Athletic Conference champions and an at-large opponent. But ramifications of this contest extend beyond the blue turf of Bronco Stadium. Before the game, hundreds of area youth are treated to an inspirational breakfast program and autograph session with leading athletes. Local companies pick up the tab for that event and for the kids' football tickets. It's all part of an effort to emphasize that there is more to sports than winning a game. The "H" Bowl matchup takes its name from the Boise-based effort to salute big-name athletes who evidence world-class kindness. Each year, the World Sports Humanitarian Hall of Fame inducts leading sports figures—Chi Chi Rodriguez, Kevin Johnson, Jim Plunkett, A.C. Green, and the like. These are sports celebrities who also do "good and noble things." Mirroring that positive spirit, the organization also recognizes a representative from each Humanitarian Bowl team for charitable efforts on and off the field.

A white Christmas is a special treat in the City of Trees. Although over 200 inches of snow fall annually in nearby mountain areas, Boise's average winter temperature of 39 degrees is too warm for snow. Many families gladly make a mountain trek to cut the holiday tree. *Photo © David R. Frazier Photolibrary*

> "Here at John L. Scott Real Estate, we have helped thousands of people make a smooth transition into a new northwest community. We feel that it is extremely important for new families to not only find a home that meets their needs, but a neighborhood that makes you feel at home inside a community with all the amenities that are important to you. Fortunately, Boise is home to dozens of neighborhoods offering the best in Americana standards."
>
> **Craig Groves**
> **President**
> **John L. Scott Real Estate**

After the game, Boiseans take to the streets and area art venues for a family-friendly First Night celebration. Sponsored by the Boise City Arts Commission, the event offers exhibits, performances, and plenty of opportunities for participation in events that range from face painting to parades in an alcohol-free environment.

With the New Year, Idaho lawmakers return to the State House. The imposing capitol building symbolizes Boise's role as the hub of Idaho government. It also reflects the city's unique position at the forefront of Western progress. As the largest metropolitan area between Salt Lake City, Utah and Portland, Oregon, and the site of federal offices, Boise leads the region in government, business, medicine, education, and government. The community's involvement in endeavors beyond the Gem State is apparent at the bustling airport. This is a global community in the Intermountain West. It's no wonder that Boiseans possess a great affinity for culture, politics, and current affairs.

Each winter, Boiseans with a penchant for prose and poetry attend readings and workshops at the Log Cabin Literary Center. Theater lovers enjoy Broadway road shows at the Morrison Center for the Performing Arts. At schools throughout the valley, learning continues into the evening. Community Education Classes teach

The Rainbow Bridge, built by Works Progress Administration crews during the 1930s, is a picturesque Payette River landmark any time of year. The still-functional span, about an hour's drive north of Boise, is especially lovely in winter. *Photo © David R. Frazier Photolibrary*

Boise's public buildings and private homes become festive displays of light and color during the holiday season. *Photo © Troy Maben/Idaho Stock Images*

everything from household skills and handicrafts to fine arts and foreign languages.

In January, thousands fill the Boise State Pavilion to hear lectures about the importance of diversity during Martin Luther King, Jr./Idaho Human Rights Day Celebrations. During February, people of all backgrounds celebrate Black History, and local celebrity artists raise awareness and support for the fight against AIDS by creating special valentines.

In the Treasure Valley, citizens enjoy the best of divergent worlds. While snowplows seldom get a workout in the City of Trees, Boise's situation at the foothills of the Rockies offers ready access to deep powder and all the fun it brings. Snowboarders and alpine skiers take to the slopes of Bogus Basin Ski Resort just sixteen miles north of Boise. It includes 2,600 acres of skiable terrain. Ninety acres are open at night. There are groomed cross-country trails, too. Nordic skiers also find ample room to glide across the public lands surrounding Idaho City, McCall, and other mountain towns. Skaters enjoy Idaho Ice World's public rink. Hockey fans cheer the West Coast Hockey League's Steelheads at the Bank of America Center. Boise State basketball draws crowds to the Pavilion. In winter, restaurants, clubs, theaters and other city-style amenities are enhanced by the friendly charm of this place. Those advantages continue throughout the year. In every season, Boise, Idaho is a wonderful place to call home.

Each year, Boise's professional dance company, Ballet Idaho, includes talented area ballet students in a lavish presentation of *The Nutcracker*. The holiday favorite continues to delight area families with performances at the elegant 2,000-seat Velma V. Morrison Center for the Performing Arts. *Photo by Kent Peterson, courtesy of Ballet Idaho*

For many Boise families a trip to the mountains to find the perfect Christmas tree is a long-standing tradition. *Photos this page © David R. Frazier Photolibrary; (Opposite) Photo © Troy Maben/Idaho Stock Images*

Seasons of Boise

This woman enjoys schussing down the slopes at Bogus Basin while others enjoy tree-lined thoroughfares on the resort's cross-country trails. Although sledding and snow tubing are not allowed on the ski mountain, there are plenty of side roads and paths on the way to Bogus Basin. Local kids can always find a place to go for a slide. *(Opposite) Photo © Kevin Syms/David Frazier Photolibrary; (Above) Photo © David R. Frazier Photolibrary*

Part Two

Photo © Steve Bly/Idaho Stock Images

6

Manufacturing, Distribution, High Technology & Communications

Hewlett-Packard, 98

DIRECTV Boise Customer Contact Center, 100

Building Materials Holding Corporation, 101

Time Warner Telecom, 102

Photo © David R. Frazier Photolibrary

Hewlett-Packard

Invention and innovation have always been the keys to success at Hewlett-Packard.

The company was founded by Bill Hewlett and Dave Packard in a Palo Alto, California, garage in 1939. The two gentlemen were firmly in agreement with their company vision of bringing people together to work with technology in order to make a significant difference in the world. That commitment became what is now widely known as the HP Way. As Bill Hewlett once described it: "It's policies and actions that flow from the belief that men and women want to do a good job, a creative job, and that if they are provided the proper environment they will do so. Closely coupled with this is the tradition of treating each individual with consideration and respect and recognizing individual achievements."

HP operates with a focus on seven interrelated corporate objectives that promote success in the ever-changing world of the technology industry—profit, customers, fields of interest, growth, our people, management, and citizenship. Each objective builds upon the others to create a comprehensive plan.

Profit is, of course, the cornerstone of any successful business. A company must wisely manage its profits in banner years to continue operations during slower, more cautious days. Sound asset management provides HP with the means to maintain a consistent level of activity and progress as it moves forward into the future. Successful profit management also ensures that HP customers continue to find available the highest quality products at an outstanding value.

Which leads into the next tenant of HP success—the development of a long-term relationship with satisfied customers who

Hewlett-Packard company founders David (Dave) Packard (left) and William (Bill) R. Hewlett in 1973. They adapted an innovative management style that became the "HP Way" and practiced Management by Walking Around or MBWA.

return again and again as new advances in technology warrant an update of user systems. HP strives always to meet or exceed customer expectations with an unbending commitment to quality, thereby assuring return customers.

"Fields of interest" refers to HP's broad vision toward the future of the technology industry, addressed by the company's research and development arm. HP's basic purpose is "to accelerate the advancement of knowledge and fundamentally improve the effectiveness of individuals and organizations." HP's researchers build on their knowledge of existing technology with a vision toward anticipating new customer and industry needs and desires. They strive to look beyond what we know to anticipate what we need to know.

This visioning process leads directly into the next facet—growth. In an industry as dynamic as the technology field, a company cannot remain static without quickly losing significant ground. With the globalization of the marketplace in the technology sector, HP must establish a presence that inspires confidence in customers around the world to choose its product, and that draws the best and brightest to work for HP, perpetuating a strong future.

HP employees are encouraged to work independently to achieve overall objectives of the company as a whole. This emphasis on individual accomplishment helps foster an environment where new ideas are readily proposed and tested and risks taken that just might open the door to another world.

HP is a leading global provider of products, technologies, solutions, and services to consumers and businesses. The company's offerings span IT infrastructure, personal computing and access devices, global services, and imaging and printing.

By providing its people with a flexible and dynamic workplace, HP builds long-term relationships with employees. The HP management style encourages independent thought that results in a wellspring of new ideas and that fits perfectly with the unconventional nature of a cutting-edge industry that is like no other. HP is in the business of manufacturing ideas, as much as any hardware, service, or technical software.

Finally, HP strives to impact local communities in which its many offices and facilities are located throughout the world by reaching out with volunteers and financial support of non-profit organizations and educational institutions in the community.

HP came to Boise in 1973 to operate a disc drive manufacturing facility that provided jobs for hundreds of local residents. In 1984, HP Boise employees pioneered the first LaserJet printer, which is often referred to as the "crown jewel" of the company. Today, the employees are dedicated to research and development, general business, manufacturing, and customer support for IT infrastructure, services, and imaging and printing products for a global marketplace.

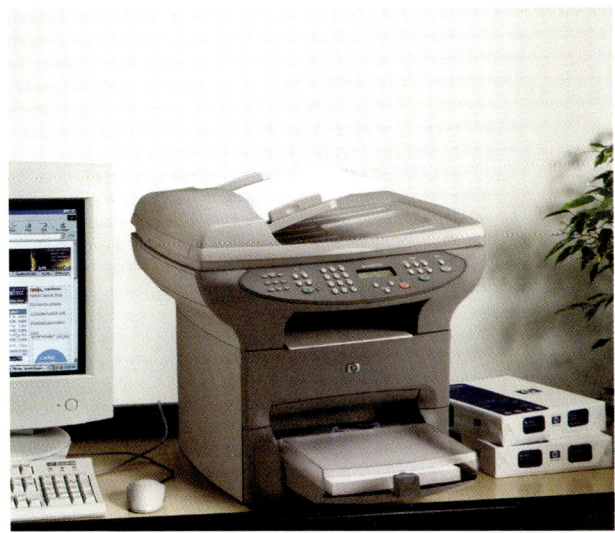

In 1994 HP introduced the first multi-function device. Today the printer-copier-scanner streamlines communications for small businesses and home offices by providing full-featured laser printing, copying, and color scanning in a single device. Businesses gain productivity and professionalism with this affordable, space saving solution.

The HP Boise operations occupy more than 2 million square feet of office space in four Boise locations including the main site on 220 acres of land eight miles west of downtown Boise. Ten percent of the facility is dedicated to state-of-the-art manufacturing operations for the imaging and printing supplies business.

Being an economic, intellectual, and social asset to the community at large is a priority at HP Boise. The company serves as one of the largest private employers in Idaho and maintains a significant community contributions program as well as a very active employee base. In any given year, HP Boise gives more than $2 million back to the community between its employee charitable giving program and corporate philanthropy through cash and equipment gifts. As a leader in building a more inclusive community, the company also has played an active role in supporting the development of the Hispanic Cultural Center of Idaho, the Idaho Black History Museum, and the Idaho Human Rights Education Center.

The future possibilities and uses for technology are limitless. With a focus on new and emerging markets while continuing to bring innovative, useful, and significant products and services to the market, HP anticipates worlds of opportunities. At HP, there are no boundaries to the future of technology. ■

HP's fundamental goal is to build positive, long-term relationships with customers, relationships characterized by mutual respect, by courtesy and integrity, by a helpful, effective response to customer needs and concerns, and by a strong commitment to providing products and services of the highest quality, value, and usefulness.

DIRECTV Boise Customer Contact Center

Millions of Americans nationwide have shown a preference for DIRECTV as their choice for home entertainment—and with good reason.

DIRECTV offers a quality digital signal, excellent programming choices, convenience and viewing control, as well as programming that is not available through any other video provider. It is these facts that have helped make DIRECTV the nation's largest provider of digital multi-channel video programming.

Viewed in one out of every nine television homes in the United States, DIRECTV offers more than 225 channels of news, information, movies, sports, family programming, high definition, and foreign language programming.

The DIRECTV System, comprised of an 18-inch satellite dish, a set-top receiver, and remote control, was the fastest-selling product in the history of consumer electronics when it was first introduced in 1994. DIRECTV beams its TV signals directly to homes from multiple satellites positioned 22,300 miles from Earth.

As home to the DIRECTV Boise Customer Contact Center, the city of Boise plays an important role in the success of DIRECTV. Beginning customer service operations in 1996 for a national cable company, the Boise Customer Contact Center was purchased by DIRECTV in 1999. This state-of-the-art call center is one of the largest private employers in the area with approximately 1,300 employees on the company payroll. The Boise Customer Contact Center is the first DIRECTV owned and operated call center, serving a nationwide customer base of more than 10.7 million customers.

As one of the largest call centers in Idaho, this 155,000-square-foot facility is positioned on a 12-acre site with its design based on innovative, best-in-class call centers from around the country. Incorporating the European ideal of "green architecture," employees at the Boise Customer Contact Center work in a comfortable environment, which in turn makes them happier and more productive

Natural light, greenery, and a water fountain in the atrium are part of the "green architecture" that creates a comfortable atmosphere for employees to work in.

and ultimately results in a positive customer service experience for the customers of DIRECTV. This concept is utilized throughout the building and includes an atrium with palm trees and a water fountain that provides white noise designed to soothe and reduce the stress levels of employees. An on-site cafeteria, fitness center, 250-seat theater, four training rooms, and a multi-functional teleconference room all feature state-of-the-art fixtures and equipment.

When the Boise Customer Contact Center was first built in 1996, it was one of the first call centers in the area. Since then, the call center industry in Boise has grown significantly and is gaining respect as a major local industry due to the strong work ethic of its citizens.

With its innovative design, the DIRECTV Boise Customer Contact Center has become one of the true giants in its industry, earning the respect and admiration of its peers in what is quickly becoming one of Boise's most competitive fields.

DIRECTV Boise Customer Contact Center.

Building Materials Holding Corporation

Chances are good that if you see a new house being built around Boise, Building Materials Holding Corporation (BMHC) had something to do with the construction. BMHC is one of the leading providers of manufactured and engineered building components and construction services to the residential and light commercial builders and contractors in the West, with 58 building materials centers with 133 facilities, commonly known as BMC West, strategically placed throughout the western part of the nation.

One of the many reasons contractors turn to BMHC for their building needs is that the company assists its customers with full-service capabilities, including building materials and the offering of more manufactured and engineered building components and construction services than its competitors. BMHC has earned respect and admiration from its clients by offering superior service from knowledgeable employees and prompt delivery of products. BMHC considers its sales force to be the best in the market today, based on the fact that its sales people understand how a building is constructed and the requirements of each project. Each project presented to the sales people receives the same amount of care, knowledge, and scrutiny as the next one.

BMC West was founded in Boise in 1987 by management members Don Hendrickson, Steve Pearson, Ellis Goebel, and Dick Blackwood as part of a leverage buyout of Boise Cascade's retail distribution division. Since 1997, the company has expanded from the lumberyard business by adding more manufactured and engineered building components and construction services such as roof and floor trusses and pre-hung doors. Recently, BMHC acquired a framing business that has proven to be beneficial to the success of the corporation, allowing the builder to not only get the framing packages that BMHC has always offered, but also the doors, trusses, and even framers to help frame the packages. BMHC is one of the first companies of its kind to acquire a framing company and utilize it as part of the business, which has helped propel it into becoming one of the true leaders in its field.

BMHC offers construction services and building products to professional homebuilders, including the creation of customized building materials packages, truss design, manufacturing and framing, and other installation services.

At BMHC, the goals are to continue growing and holding steadfast to its reputation as the premier building materials and building service suppliers in the west. BMHC will continue to focus on tailoring its manufactured and engineered building components and construction services to meet the needs of its knowledgeable professional customers.

BMHC has become the success story that it is today by offering innovative services and manufactured and engineered building components from experienced sales people. By staying true to its commitments to its customers, the possibilities for BMHC's growth will prove to be endless.

BMHC maintains a strong focus on superior customer service and provides expert logistical capabilities and coordinated, on-time job site delivery of building materials.

Time Warner Telecom

As technology continues to astound us all on a daily basis, one company is fully prepared for the future of technology and the future of Boise. Time Warner Telecom (TWTC) is a leading provider of local and regional optical networks and broadband services acting as a facility-based communications carrier for the businesses of Boise.

Coming to the city in 2001 after TWTC picked up the assets of GST Communications, TWTC's business model is to sell the last mile broadband connection to businesses by delivering communications services. These services include voice services, Internet access, data, and transport services delivered not only to the local market but also to 43 other markets around the country. The company came to Boise after determining that it didn't have a strong presence in the west. TWTC then picked up the assets in Boise after looking at the town and businesses here. The company noticed the high growth, high technology, and highly educated market that will cause these services to be even more in demand in the future. In just a short time, TWTC was able to land several major accounts in the city including HP, Micron PC, Micron Technology, Boise State University, and the City of Boise. By bringing in creativity and capabilities that were new to the city, TWTC has been able to help its clients save money and get better quality service that supports their every need.

Stand-alone AC and DC power provide reliable, efficient service.

Currently with less than 30 employees in Boise, Time Warner Telecom is small and agile enough to adapt to what its customers want and need, yet large enough to command and deliver services across the country as a financially solvent entity. With its presence now firmly entrenched in the city, Boise has received a glimpse of what TWTC can offer its clients that its competitors cannot. Upon arrival, TWTC upgraded most of its fiber-based equipment to increase its available bandwidth and brought new services with them to Boise. The company is able to sell Ethernet based access over the network as well as FiberChannel and ESCON, which interconnects IBM mainframes. By expanding its networks in the market and continuously upgrading its products and services offered, Time Warner Telecom has become the natural choice as a communications provider for businesses, whether it is voice, data, transport, or Internet.

With unrivaled technical expertise and financial stability, TWTC will continue to have a positive impact on and become a major support to the growth and development of Boise. When businesses deal with Time Warner Telecom they understand that they are employing the services of a major telecommunicator who can not only take care of their every need today, but will continue to do so far into the future. ■

Time Warner Telecom has state-of-the-art equipment providing 800Gb of availability to the Boise market.

Photo © David R. Frazier Photolibrary

7

Business & Finance

United Heritage, 106

The Boise Metro Chamber of Commerce, 110

Wells Fargo, 112

KeyBank, 113

Great West Casualty Company, 114

Photo © Steve Bly / Idaho Stock Images

United Heritage

Everyone has hopes and dreams for the future. For many, those hopes and dreams include not only personal financial security but also the financial security of their family once they depart this world. At United Heritage, we try to make those dreams a reality for our policyholders and clients. No matter what your situation may be, United Heritage has the products that will help you realize your hopes and dreams.

Based in Meridian, United Heritage specializes in the sale, underwriting, and service of quality life insurance, fixed annuities, financial products, and property and casualty insurance. Each of its companies strives to maintain strong financial positions for the protection, security, and benefit for their clients.

The company was incorporated as "Grange Mutual Life Company" in Nampa in 1934. Two Idahoans were the primary founders of this Idaho financial company. W.W. Deal was the chief organizer and initiator of the company, and the first president was Charles S. Taylor, both natives of Nampa. Grange Mutual was originally licensed to offer affordable life insurance only to Grange members living in Washington and Idaho.

Expansion followed soon thereafter. In 1944, the company began selling insurance in Oregon, Montana, and Colorado. By 1958, the company eliminated the Grange membership requirement and opened its doors to the general public. One year later, the states of Wyoming, California, and Iowa were added to the company's licensed business area. Arizona and Nevada followed in 1970, South Dakota in

Richard E. Hall, Chairman of the Board, United Heritage Mutual Holding/Financial Group/Life Insurance Company.

1971, and Utah in 1972. By the end of 1991, the company had added nine additional states to its ever-growing territory and was by then offering coverage to people in all 22 continental states west of the Mississippi River.

It was in that same year, 1991, that Grange Mutual Life Company officially changed its name to United Heritage Mutual Life Insurance Company. The company chose the name United Heritage to memorialize its new status as a regional insurer, dedicated to providing quality life insurance to residents of the American heartland and the west. To further reflect its image as a strong, vibrant insurer, the company adopted as its new logo an American bald eagle in flight. Today the company has over 1200 life insurance agents in a 22+ state area.

By the early 1990s, several of the company's life insurance agents were beginning to add financial planning to their life insurance sales. At the same time, United Heritage's policyholders wanted to expand their investment alternatives. In response to the needs of its agents and policyholders in the fast-changing world of personal finance, the company created United Heritage Financial Services, an NASD general securities broker-dealer, to market equity products such as mutual funds and variable insurance products in 1994. United Heritage Financial Services became the first retail broker-dealer domiciled in the state of Idaho. Today, over 100 registered representatives are contracted with United Heritage Financial Services in 23 states,

Dennis L. Johnson, President and CEO, United Heritage Mutual Holding/Financial Group/Life Insurance Company.

Jack J. Winderl, President and CEO, United Heritage Financial Services; Executive Vice President, Investments; and Treasurer, United Heritage Mutual Holding/Financial Group/Life Insurance Company.

providing clients with the access to over 50 Mutual Fund families, 40 Variable Annuity carriers, 10 Variable Universal Life issuers, and four limited partnership programs. United Heritage Financial Services also offers full stock, corporate and municipal bond investment opportunities, options, mutual funds, variable life, annuities, 401(k)s, and investment advisory services.

In 2000, United Heritage again expanded its product and service portfolio when it became the majority and subsequently sole shareholder of Idaho's oldest insurance company (1908) and the foremost writer of fire insurance in the state. The former Idaho Mutual Insurance Company was demutualized and joined United Heritage. After the acquisition, the first in company history, United Heritage Property & Casualty Company joined United Heritage Mutual Life and United Heritage Financial Services in the United Heritage family of companies, providing property and casualty insurance due to fire, weather, liability, and business interruption to the residents of the state of Idaho. There are 85 agencies in Idaho alone, and it expanded into Oregon during 2002.

In 2001, in response to new federal and state laws that blur the lines between financial institutions and which allow mutual insurers more flexibility in capital acquisition, United Heritage Mutual Life took the necessary steps to convert its corporate structure from that of a mutual insurance company to a new structure called a "mutual holding company." With its policyholders' overwhelming approval, a new parent company, United Heritage Mutual Holding Company,

Main Entrance, United Heritage Building.

was created to replace United Heritage Mutual Life Insurance Company as the "top" company in the corporate structure. United Heritage Mutual Holding Company is owned by the policyholders of the life insurance company, and is the sole shareholder of United Heritage Financial Group. United Heritage Financial Group, in turn, owns the stock of United Heritage Life Insurance Company, United Heritage Property & Casualty Company, and United Heritage Financial Services. This new structure will allow United Heritage the flexibility to acquire additional companies and more easily raise capital.

In addition to this change in corporate structure, 2001 saw United Heritage experience its first change of address since the early 1960s. In July of 2001, United Heritage moved its operations into a new, state-of-the art home office adjacent to Interstate 84 in Meridian that reigns as one of the most technologically advanced buildings in the state. This new home is designed to allow the company to grow in the upcoming years and is capable of utilizing several technological breakthroughs, including fiber optic technology to each desktop, high-speed T-1 Internet access, smart boards, plasma displays, and the ability to videoconference with anyone, anywhere.

United Heritage is much more than brick and mortar, however. The quality and depth of experience of its current management team is typified by President and CEO, Dennis L. Johnson. Mr. Johnson began his career with United Heritage in 1983 and successively occupied the positions of general counsel, corporate secretary, executive vice president, and chief operating officer of United

Sculpture in lobby representing the United Heritage corporate logo.

Heritage Life before becoming president and CEO in January of 1999. In addition, Mr. Johnson was one of the founders of United Heritage Financial Services and served as its president and CEO

United Heritage Corporate Headquarters.

Brian E. Henman, President and CEO, United Heritage Property & Casualty Company.

until 1999. Over thirty percent of the company's current work force has been with the company over 20 years, which translates into over 600 years of insurance industry experience. United Heritage is a family-friendly employer that also helps its employees with financial assistance to achieve academic goals.

United Heritage's main focus, however, is on its policyholders and clients. Through the years, the company has remained dedicated to providing the highest quality insurance products and service to its customers. For those young policyholders who have recently married or are starting a family, United Heritage offers Permanent Life and Term Life insurance plans. In addition to providing lifetime insurance coverage, permanent life also contains a savings element designed to assist with future financial needs. Term life offers low cost life insurance that provides protection for a specified period of time.

For those policyholders and clients with established careers and a need for financial security, United Heritage Financial Services offers mutual funds, stocks, variable annuities, and bonds. Through United Heritage Life, a policyholder can purchase universal life products, which combine a monthly-adjusted interest rate and a form of monthly purchased term insurance, which keeps the product sensitive to changes in the economy. Finally, homeowner's and small business protection is provided through United Heritage Property & Casualty.

Planning for retirement can be a trying period for many people. However, United Heritage can help make the transition into the twilight years much smoother with its wide array of products designed to assist retirees get the most for their money. In addition to universal life products, United Heritage Life has funeral pre-planning products designed specifically to be used for the funding of pre-arranged funerals. Fixed annuities are also available through United Heritage Life. These annuities can be long-term savings plans, or may provide the policyholder with a constant stream of income that is guaranteed for the rest of the policyholder's life, no matter how long that policyholder may live.

While providing each client with impeccable service may be the primary goal of the United Heritage family, remaining active in the community is just as important to the company and each of its more than 100 employees. United Heritage has accomplished this goal by not only supporting and encouraging its employees to volunteer their time and efforts in worthwhile causes, such as Paint the Town, but United Heritage itself often donates funds to assist various charitable groups and entities. While there have been several organizations over the years that have benefited from United Heritage's generosity, some of the more notable recipients include the United Way, the Boy Scouts, the Women's Alliance, the American Red Cross, and Junior Achievement. The year 2002 found United Heritage forming a relationship with the Idaho Community Foundation, which resulted in the newly created United Heritage Fund, a philanthropic gift fund. This fund is non-endowed as well as fully expendable and can be used to distribute monetary donations to any IRS recognized charity at any time.

United Heritage complements its charitable efforts with corporate sponsorship of local community events. In January of 2002, United Heritage helped the city of Boise put together the best Olympic Torch Relay Celebration in the United States. The celebration was such a success that the city of Boise was awarded only one of four Olympic cauldrons in the world that are found outside of Olympic headquarters. As a show of appreciation for United Heritage's sponsorship of the award-winning celebration, the company was granted the opportunity to be the first host of the Olympic Cauldron upon its arrival in Boise. United Heritage's contribution to this event shows not only its commitment to the community, but its pride in helping to promote an important occasion that will be looked upon fondly by residents of the Treasure Valley for many years to come.

Simply put, United Heritage has successfully positioned itself on the cusp of the latest trends in the financial services and insurance industries in order to remain at the top of its field during the upcoming century. When looking for a company that is large enough to meet your financial needs, yet small enough to offer personalized and friendly service, with a strong commitment to its clients as well as its community, look to United Heritage. United Heritage—for the life you deserve.

The Boise Metro Chamber of Commerce

The Boise Metro Chamber of Commerce is the oldest and largest general business organization in the state and has a long history of serving the needs of businesses. The Chamber was incorporated in 1885, five years before the Idaho Territory achieved statehood. For over 116 years, the Chamber has served its community as the principal advocate for the area's business community, dedicated to enhancing the economic vitality of the region.

Today, the Chamber is made up of more than 4,600 individuals, representing over 1,800 member companies and organizations of all sizes in the Boise Metropolitan Statistical Area (MSA), which includes Ada and Canyon counties. The Chamber concentrates its focus on economic development, advocacy, community betterment, small business support, and creating opportunities for the business community to have a voice in the area's present and future development.

Central to the Chamber's mission is its role as the "Advocate for the Business Community." The Chamber serves as the voice of businesses of all sizes; working on their behalf with elected officials at all levels of government—from the highway district to the state legislature. With the Chamber's governmental affairs division acting as a full-time lobbyist, companies can be sure that issues important to business are being supported.

As the only regional chamber of commerce in the state, the Boise Metro Chamber plays a key role in facilitating partnerships between business, government, education, and other chambers for a regional approach to the issues affecting the entire Treasure Valley. For the past nine years, the Chamber has brought together business leaders with government officials and educators at an annual Leadership Conference. Past conferences have focused on

"Wings over Boise" is a public art piece on the parking structure at the Boise Airport. The garage will soon be connected to a new $100 million airport terminal. *Photo by Ken Schneider*

the issues of transportation, education, workforce development, and responsible growth, and have resulted in a number of partnerships, programs, and initiatives vital to the successful growth of the city.

The Boise Metro Economic Development Council (BMEDC), a Chamber division, is the leading regional economic development organization involving both public and private partners. The council recently facilitated a collaborated effort between the area's call centers and Boise State University to create a first-of-its-kind Customer Care Specialist Program at the University's Selland College of Technology. This new certificate program serves as a model for similar programs across the country. In the past, the Chamber played a significant role in the establishment of the College of Engineering at Boise State University to help meet the needs of the area's hi-tech sector.

Boise is not only an ideal place to visit, but is the perfect place to work, raise a family, and make a home—and the Chamber is dedicated to keeping it that way. The Boise Metro Chamber of Commerce is involved in all aspects of the area's growth and development. From transportation improvements to development issues to matters surrounding education and workforce development, the voice of the Chamber is sought, heard, and respected throughout the region and the state.

The Chamber seeks to keep its membership engaged and active

Sunset in downtown Boise. The unique beauty of the foothills serves as a backdrop to Idaho's Capitol. *Photo by Pat Teglia, Teglia Photography*

through its many programs and services. Monthly networking events, affordable training, trade shows, and community events, such as the Boise Mayor's State of the City Address and the annual Economic Outlook Forum, are just some of the opportunities available. Chamber members can lend their voice to the decision making process through participation in one of the Chamber's many committees and task forces on such issues as education, transportation, and local, state, and federal government.

With over 75 percent of the Chamber's membership made up of small and medium-sized businesses, the Chamber understands how important small businesses are to Boise's economy. That's why the Chamber honors the valuable contributions that small businesses make to the area at the annual Small Business of the Year Awards luncheon. Quarterly trade shows and after hours events provide many affordable networking opportunities for small business entrepreneurs.

The Chamber's Leadership Boise Program has been training civic and community leaders for over 25 years, and is a model for programs of its kind across the country.

In the 1980s, the Chamber collaborated with public and private entities to create a downtown urban renewal program that resulted in the creation of the Downtown Boise Association. Since 1987, the Downtown Boise Association, a business improvement district, has worked to revitalize the downtown core. Working proactively to promote Boise as a clean, safe, and vibrant place to live, the Downtown Boise Association has helped make the city one of the premier places in the country to live.

Boiseans enjoy a summer day on the Greenbelt, a paved, 25-mile path running along the Boise River. *Photo by Pat Teglia, Teglia Photography*

With 116 years of dedicated service behind it, the Boise Metro Chamber is looking ahead to the next 100 years. Because Boise is considered a high-tech city with many technology companies and start-ups, and has a diversified economy, a highly skilled workforce, and a strong entrepreneurial environment, it entered the global marketplace much faster than other cities of similar size. The Boise Metro Chamber is already working on the partnerships, infrastructure, and sense of place that will establish Boise as a key player in the borderless economy of the future.

Above all else, collaboration is the key to the Boise Metro Chamber of Commerce's success. The Chamber has the unique ability to bring the public and private sectors together and establish partnerships that work. Together, these partnerships identify strengths, weaknesses, and solutions for the community and region. ■

The Grove, a plaza in the heart of downtown, is host to public art and many of the city's festivals and events. *Photo by Steve Bly, Steve Bly Photography*

Wells Fargo

Wells Fargo was founded on the American frontier to satisfy a fundamental need—connecting one customer to another in one market after another by transporting goods and services fast and securely across great distances.

The company is still on that journey that began in 1852, which is reflected in the company's vision: To satisfy all of its customers' financial needs and help them succeed financially. Wells Fargo wants to be recognized by its customers as the premier provider of financial services—number one, second to none.

To its individual and business customers, who have entrusted the company with their business, this means building a financial partnership; providing sound and professional financial advice; offering a broad, comprehensive array of products and services; providing access to any channel that its customers choose, when they choose; offering more convenience, and rewarding its customers for giving Wells Fargo its business.

How can Wells Fargo satisfy all of its customers' needs and help them succeed financially? While the world is a lot more complex than it was in 1852, connecting is still the company's rallying cry. Wells Fargo unites with its clients to transfer information and wealth. The company joins with its customers on an emotional level as well by caring and taking the time to listen, questioning the customer, and connecting their answer to the proper products and service. The client is also connected to its business partners, such as investments and insurance, so customer goals can be matched with the best financial service strategies.

One of the most important ways the company connects with its customers is through its people. At Wells Fargo, the company's greatest competitive advantage is its people. Products and technology can be copied and prices can be beat. But it's the people who

Wells Fargo's vision is to satisfy all of its customers' financial needs and help them to succeed financially. *Photo courtesy of Andrew Rafkind Photography*

set Wells Fargo apart from its competitors and who strengthen and deepen relationships with the customers.

Wells Fargo is only as healthy and prosperous as the communities that it serves. It is dedicated to the communities in which its people live and work and actively supports areas including economic development, education, economic self-sufficiency, social services, and the arts. In Idaho, Wells Fargo contributes a percentage of its profits each year to the community so that everyone can share in its growth and success.

Wells Fargo celebrated its 150th birthday in 2002. While much has changed since 1852, the company's commitment is constant. With almost 2,000 team members and more than 100 banking locations in the state, Idaho can count on Wells Fargo to continue as its customers' steadfast partner in promoting growth and prosperity.

Wells Fargo is a diversified financial services company providing banking, insurance, investments, mortgage, and consumer finance through more than 100 store locations in Idaho. *Photo courtesy of Andrew Rafkind Photography*

KeyBank

When Alexander Younie, a Canadian-born Scotsman, immigrated to Idaho in the 1840s and opened the First National Bank of Blackfoot in 1905, he couldn't have imagined that the community bank he founded and successfully managed through the depression of the 1920s would ultimately become part of one of the nation's largest banking companies. But that's exactly what happened. His son-in-law Neil Boyle took over as bank president after Younie's death, and following a series of successful mergers, First National Bank of Blackfoot found its way into the KeyBank family.

Today, Key brings to Idaho much of the same commitment that helped make Younie's community bank a success during such turbulent economic times. By combining the capital and resources of a national financial services company with the delivery infrastructure and market understanding of a local company, Key is able to fill the needs for its services that continue to impact the state's economy.

Key, for example, has maintained its strong support of agribusiness, demonstrating its understanding of local market conditions and the state's reliance on the agricultural sector. In spite of the sector's ups and downs, Key has continued lending in the ag industry well beyond its composite base and delivers top quality services and products to its clients, developing a relationship as a trusted advisor.

Beyond that commitment, Key has been instrumental in bringing world-class products to Idaho, delivering large corporate-type products to a smaller market. Everything from investment banking to cash management, insurance, Internet and online banking services, commercial banking and finance, foreign exchange and international banking are handled under the Key umbrella. In fact, many of the services Key provides in Idaho would simply not be available without Key's presence and support.

Community Support Remains Strong

Recognizing the importance of well-established community services, Key strives to have a positive impact on each community

KeyBank's corporate office in Idaho is located in the heart of downtown Boise.

in which it operates. Locally, several charities benefit from Key's generous support through employee volunteerism and direct contributions. Each year, Key sponsors its "Neighbors Make a Difference Day" program where the company closes nearly all of its branches and offices and employees spend the afternoon working on more than 1,000 community projects around the country.

Organizations such as the Boys and Girls Clubs, YMCA, Zoo Boise, March of Dimes, the Women's and Children's Alliance, the Discovery Center of Idaho, the Idaho Women's Fitness Celebration, and the Idaho Shakespeare Festival have all been recipients of the goodwill that Key and its employees share with the community.

By delivering world-class financial services and products with a local delivery system using local people, Key will continue to produce winning numbers for its shareholders, employees, and clients. When combined with its continued high profile in the community, Key is poised to serve as a valued ambassador to the city well into the future.

Key's newest branch office in Eagle, Idaho. In Idaho, Key has 30 branch offices statewide.

Great West Casualty Company

Great West Casualty Company is a specialty insurance company that provides property and casualty coverage for the trucking industry, specifically long-haul trucks for hire and freight companies. The company's mission is to be "the" premier provider of insurance products and services for truckers, and it accomplishes this by understanding each of its customers' service needs and providing for those needs, meeting and exceeding all expectations.

The company first got its start in South Sioux City, Nebraska in 1936 when the father and son team of Joseph A. and Joseph W. Morten saw an opportunity to assist truckers with gathering the necessary permits and authority in order to operate in interstate commerce. This paved the way for a business enterprise that has blossomed into one of the most respected insurance organizations in the trucking business.

In August of 1989, Great West Casualty Company opened its first regional office in Boise with a work force of 30 people. Today, that work force has more than doubled and operates as a full-service office, offering underwriting, safety, claim handling, subrogation, support, human resources, and administration services.

Great West has always been committed to the trucking industry, wishing to be viewed as its partner in enterprise. By providing financial security and protection to its members, Great West is able to experience the business from the truckers' point-of-view and is able to act in each of their best interests.

The company has been a tremendous asset to the city of Boise and the surrounding Treasure Valley by becoming an exceptional corporate citizen. A member of the Boise Area Chamber of Commerce, Great West Casualty Company also supports and participates in such activities as Paint the Town, Rake Up Boise, the Komen Walk for the Cure, the Heart Walk for the American Heart Association, and the Festival of Trees. In recent years, the organization has been recognized

Great West Casualty Company front lobby.

as one of the top five recipients of the Award of Excellence for Philanthropic Leadership by the United Way of Treasure Valley.

Today, Great West experiences continued growth and will seek to expand its partnerships and profits while maintaining the highest levels of customer service. These goals shall be accomplished by providing continuous development of quality service to its customers, owners, employees, and associates. At Great West Casualty Company, everyone involved embraces the impending heights and rewarding challenges that the future will bring.

Great West Casualty Company Western Regional Office.

Photo © Patrick Teglia

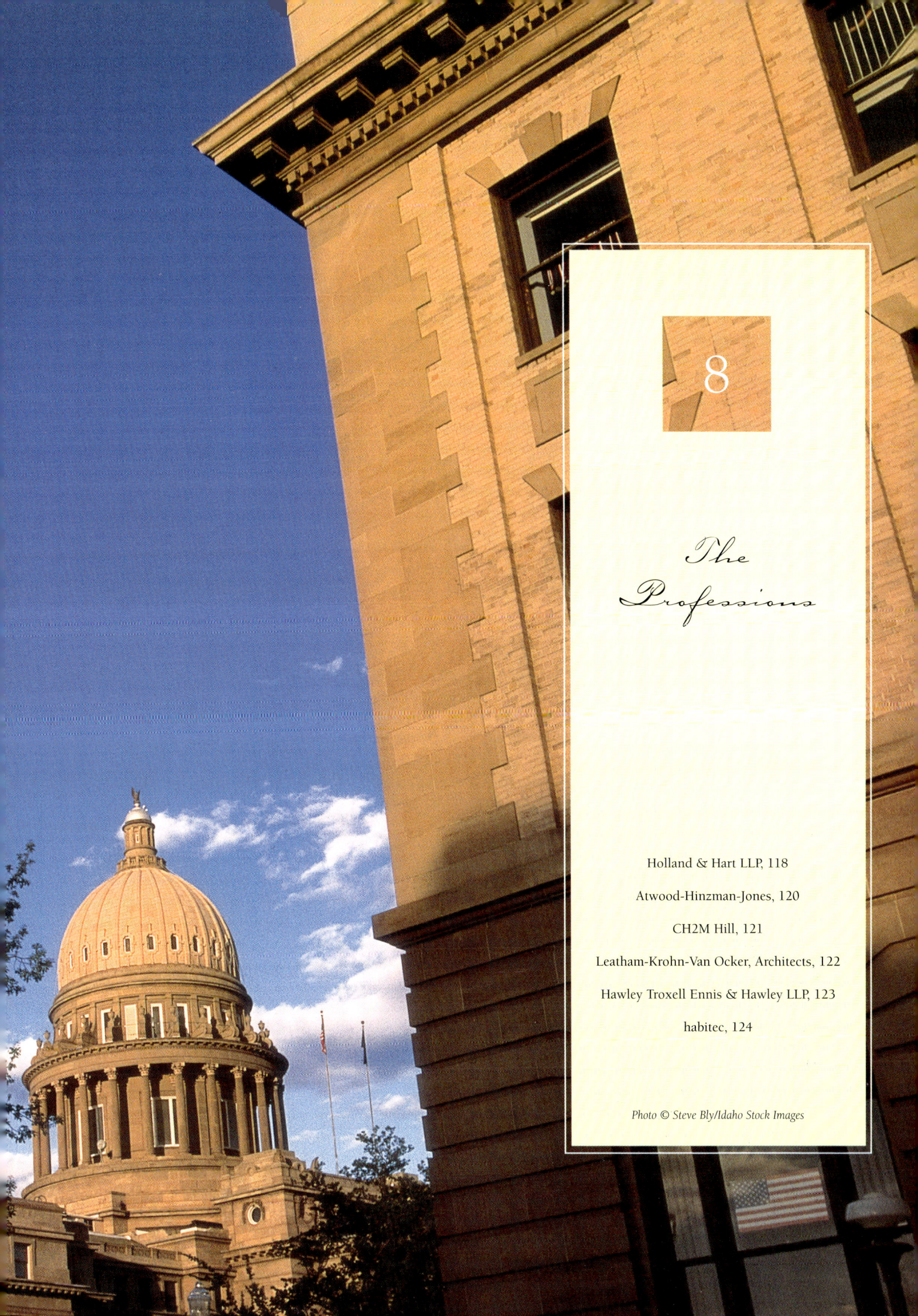

8

The Professions

Holland & Hart LLP, 118

Atwood-Hinzman-Jones, 120

CH2M Hill, 121

Leatham-Krohn-Van Ocker, Architects, 122

Hawley Troxell Ennis & Hawley LLP, 123

habitec, 124

Photo © Steve Bly/Idaho Stock Images

Holland & Hart LLP

More than a decade ago it became obvious to the pioneer Idaho law firm of Langroise, Sullivan, and Smylie that Idaho's phenomenal growth would bring with it the need for sophisticated and specialized legal services. Determined to continue to provide premier legal service to Idahoans, the firm began a search that resulted in a merger with Holland & Hart, another pioneer law firm with a solid western heritage. No other law firm knows the Rocky Mountain region like Holland & Hart. Today, members of the Boise business community benefit from Holland & Hart's network of legal talent and resources that extends throughout the Rocky Mountain region.

A Rocky Mountain Law Firm With An Idaho Foundation

Founders of the Boise office include former Governor Robert Smylie, Willis Sullivan, and William Langroise. The firm's present partners are Idaho and western natives, but with varied educational and work backgrounds. They know their communities and understand the intricacies of doing business in the Rocky Mountain West. Boise clients are assured that the attorney responsible for representing their interests is a Boise attorney who is familiar with local people, customs, and rules.

Founded in 1947 by Steve Hart and Josiah Holland in Denver, Colorado, Holland & Hart's 12 offices today extend throughout Idaho, Colorado, Montana, New Mexico, Utah, Wyoming, and Washington D.C. In each geographic area, Holland & Hart's attorneys have developed a sophisticated sense of the business environment present in each region, thereby increasing the level of awareness and influence that members of the firm bring to their representation of the firm's clients. In turn, Boise clients with regional and national interests benefit from the firm's insight throughout the West and around the world.

Walter Bithell, a partner in Holland & Hart, writes a weekly column on law for the *Idaho Statesman* and is a legal analyst for KTVB-TV in Boise.

Premier Client Service

Holland & Hart's approach to the delivery of legal services is nationally recognized. First and foremost, Holland & Hart is a business law firm with a vast array of experience in the traditional areas of business practice. Firm members are experienced in a wide range of service areas, including Litigation—wrongful death, professional liability, personal injury, product liability, agriculture, business, insurance, environmental, construction; Business—growth and technology, creditor bankruptcy, banking and commercial transactions, limited liability companies, tax, employment/labor law, contracts, real estate development, estate planning; Intellectual Property—patents, trademarks, copyrights, patent

Boise clients with regional and national interests benefit from the firm's insight throughout the West and around the world.

The Law Library at Holland & Hart provides information to attorneys on a daily basis.

litigation; and Environmental—water rights, compliance, natural resources, permitting.

While excellent legal advice gives clients a huge advantage in achieving their objectives, the firm recognizes that client satisfaction extends far beyond technical competence. Clients benefit from the firm's strong commitment to the concept of client service teams, tailoring their representation to the objectives of each client.

The firm maintains an intense commitment to continually improving the level of services it provides. Because its members recognize that responsiveness, timeliness, and effective communication are all important to client service, Holland & Hart has implemented a variety of programs to use surveys, interviews, and focus groups in helping the firm understand and meet client expectations, needs, and preferences.

Leading Edge Litigation Support

With a level of service that exceeds most business law firms, Holland & Hart is also known for its experience in litigation, trials, and appeals, providing services to both defendants and plaintiffs. Holland & Hart clients are well served by the firm's ability to present clear, well-reasoned arguments to juries and judges. Furthermore, the firm is equipped with state-of-the-art technology that allows Holland & Hart attorneys in offices throughout the nation to work together as if they were side by side. Litigation support software includes full text searching tools used for witness preparation, depositions, and expert testimony. Databases track documents, exhibits, witnesses, and other information pertinent to particular cases.

Both Boise and Denver offices house a mock trial room, which is part of a trial preparation center. This replica of an actual courtroom helps attorneys and clients fine-tune the clarity of their presentations and arguments before going to trial. Each room includes videotaping capabilities that allow attorneys and clients to view mock trial proceedings in preparation for the real courtroom.

To further ensure that clients benefit from the highest quality of professional presentation, Holland & Hart maintains its own in-house graphics department. A full-time staff of artists, designers, and computer specialists enables the firm to produce the finest visual aids quickly, cost efficiently, and confidently by the Holland & Hart team.

Bottom-Line Innovation

The firm's innovative fee structure also reflects its commitment to efficiency and value. Holland & Hart is prepared to provide alternatives to hourly billing, such as contingent fees, fixed fees, or others as requested by its clients. The firm's sophisticated means of evaluating risk for clients helps them weigh the total cost of legal services against the significance of the problem. It enables clients to make an informed decision and budget for legal expenses.

Contributing Members of the Community

Holland & Hart's commitment to excellence also carries over to the communities in which its members live and work. As a firm, Holland & Hart contributes to over 150 charitable and civic causes each year. As a matter of policy, each lawyer is asked to find time to volunteer to benefit the community. Providing free legal services to those unable to pay is an obligation of each lawyer at Holland & Hart, but is by no means their only public service. Lawyers and staff alike have taken part in numerous legal, charitable, civic, and political groups. ■

Holland & Hart's mock trial room is part of the critical trial preparation. A replica of an actual courtroom helps attorneys and clients fine-tune the clarity of their presentations and arguments before going to trial.

Atwood-Hinzman-Jones

As Boise continues to prosper and grow, one local firm makes a positive impact on its future by providing a modern and innovative look to the city's architectural landscape.

Atwood-Hinzman-Jones, Inc. (AHJ) is a structural engineering consulting firm founded in 1985 by Dick Atwood, Chuck Hinzman, and Keith Jones. The three men had previously worked together in Spokane, Washington and had seen a potential for business in Boise during the early 1980s. In 1994, Jones bought out the office and has served as the corporation's president and sole supervisor of 10-20 employees over the years.

AHJ's primary customers are architects, contractors, and developers. The firm has completed work on a variety of projects over the years including commercial, institutional, retail, industrial, educational, churches, and upper-end residential homes. Their history demonstrates that there is nothing that AHJ cannot do when it comes to structural engineering consulting. This dedication and commitment has resulted in being respected by not only the firm's clients, but also the city as a whole. Through this work, AHJ has been afforded the opportunity to employ its vast experience and education in turn to educating the community and making it a better and safer place through its structures. AHJ has helped the city progress and become conscious of seismic design analysis, wind loads, and several other factors that are instrumental in helping its clients and the community become more aware of building codes in the area.

AHJ's accomplishments can be seen in several prominent structures throughout the Boise area. Some of these include the Capital Mutual Bank downtown, the Elks Rehabilitation Hospital, the renovation of the Empire Building, and the new Boise High School additions and remodeling project. AHJ has become the firm to turn to when renovating a historic building, which is evident in several structures throughout the Warehouse district downtown.

Washington Mutual Capital Plaza, Boise, Idaho.

Working together as a team and employing cutting-edge technology, AHJ offers more flexibility in the manner that jobs are approached and completed than its competitors. With a flexible approach balancing complexity with timeliness, which ensures the architectural design, AHJ proves that its strongest point is its architectural-based design approach to new projects. With a team of exuberant, bright engineers and technicians who possess the energy and desire to take structural engineering to the next level, AHJ is poised to continue making Boise a safer place to live. With 17 years of outstanding service in Idaho, AHJ continues its passion for quality and commitment to the Boise community while focusing on client satisfaction and peace of mind.

Empire Building Renovation, Boise, Idaho.

CH2M HILL

One of the oldest and most treasured businesses in Boise is CH2M HILL, which has provided service to the Treasure Valley and Idaho for more than 50 years. Although the company has 165 locations and 12,000 employees worldwide, many people are unaware that while the company was founded in Corvallis, Oregon, its second office opened in Boise in 1950. Even more interesting is that throughout its existence CH2M HILL's Boise office has only had three office managers, which has helped define a record of longevity that appeals to both customers and employees alike.

The employee owners at CH2M HILL are committed to making a difference in the quality of America's built and natural environment through people, service, and knowledge. The overall goal of the company has always been to provide competitive engineering, planning, economic, and scientific consulting services. CH2M HILL delivers projects to Idaho and the world that help public and private clients apply technology, safeguard the environment, and realize a greater return on their investment through sustainable infrastructure. Serving as a behind-the-scenes engineering firm, CH2M HILL has been involved with many of the major infrastructure projects in the valley. Among those projects are the West Boise Wastewater Treatment Facility, the Broadway-Chinden connector, the convention center, and various buildings on Boise State University's campus, including Bronco Stadium and the Velma V. Morrison Center.

CH2M HILL fully understands that the company is in the business of selling its people and the talents that each brings to bear in meeting specific challenges. Traditionally, CH2M HILL was founded on a basis of client service and applying the best possible technology on behalf of its clients. That tradition continues today. One of the company's main advantages is a commanding local presence coupled

Providing 25 years of service at the West Boise Wastewater Treatment Facility in support of Boise's growth and environmental stewardship.

with strong ties to the national firm. These ties provide its clients with access to an extensive pool of expertise and an array of services that its competitors simply cannot match.

One factor that plays a major role in the company's success is that it is employee owned. Each employee has a stake in the performance of the company, freeing it from being driven by immediate stockholder returns and providing CH2M HILL with a large advantage in the marketplace. The company is one of the largest employee-owned firms in the country and certainly the largest in its business.

The staff at CH2M HILL remain proactive in anticipating growth and are planning and designing specifically for that growth to form a healthier community through sustainable development. By playing a vital role in the community's growth and the growth in the infrastructure marketplace, CH2M HILL will help to shape Boise into an even more wonderful community for future generations.

Meeting infrastucture needs in sensitive environments.

Leatham-Krohn-Van Ocker, Architects

With each new development in science and technology the practice of architecture is reinvented. Architecture has a colorful and interesting history that spans centuries in response to its social and political surroundings. At no other architectural firm is this practice taken more to heart than at Leatham-Krohn-Van Ocker Architects.

The team of Darrell Leatham, Kent Krohn, and Amber Van Ocker combines professional experience that totals over 75 years of architectural knowledge. Darrell Leatham developed the firm in the early 60s by taking on a number of large projects and turning them into success stories. Kent Krohn began working for Leatham a decade later. They formed a partnership in 1975. Amber Van Ocker began her career under the tutelage of the two architects fresh out of architectural school in 1993. She became the third partner in 2000, bringing fresh ideas to the firm's depth of experience.

During the 38-year history of the firm, the principals have maintained a recognized practice of commercial, institutional, and private architecture, and have successfully undertaken projects with construction costs as high as fifteen million dollars.

Educational facilities have become a major component of Leatham-Krohn-Van Ocker's work. In addition to projects for Boise State University, client school districts include Basin, Emmett, Fremont, Hagerman, Hansen, Jerome, Kuna, Meridian, Middleton, Minidoka, Murtaugh, Nampa, Vallivue, and Wilder. Services range from initial project master planning and programming, through design and construction, to post-occupancy evaluations and energy audits.

Governmental agencies are also major clients of the firm, with numerous projects having been successfully completed for a variety of public entities. Client agencies included the City of Boise, the Idaho Transportation Department, the Idaho Military Division, the Idaho Department of Corrections, the Idaho Department of Parks

Century Office Building, Boise, Idaho.

and Recreation, and the Idaho Department of Administration and the Division of Public Works.

Leatham-Krohn-Van Ocker Architects have been very fortunate to have had the opportunity to work on several restoration projects at the Idaho State Capitol building. Those efforts were recognized with an AIA Honor Award for work performed on the Attorney General's Suite Reconstruction. Other design awards from the American Institute of Architects include the AIA Merit Award for the American Reserve Life Office in Boise, the Idaho First National Bank in Lewiston, and Larry Barnes Chevrolet Dealership in Boise.

Leatham-Krohn-Van Ocker's principals and highly qualified staff work directly and personally on all phases of firm projects. The firm's policy of direct principal involvement ensures that the expertise and experience of the principals is directly applied to each project. This has consistently resulted in the highest quality services for the firm's clients.

Leatham-Krohn-Van Ocker Architects is excited about the future of architecture and the Treasure Valley. The goals of the firm and the motivation of it's principals to provide experienced design and professional leadership through quality projects will create as successful a future as it has a notable past.

(Left to right) Amber Van Ocker, Darrell Leatham, and Kent Krohn standing in front of Kuna High School in Kuna, Idaho, which is currently under construction.

Hawley Troxell Ennis & Hawley LLP

The heritage of Hawley Troxell predates Idaho's statehood. The firm's legacy is so richly intertwined with Idaho's own, it is easy to overlook the fact that it is a law firm poised to meet the challenges of the 21st century with a commitment to technology, innovation, and excellence.

Idaho's largest law firm traces its origins back to James Hawley, who tried more murder cases than any other lawyer west of the Mississippi. In 1896, James Hawley and William Borah successfully handled the appeal upholding the Women's Suffrage Act in Idaho. The name Hawley has been synonymous with quality legal representation in Idaho ever since.

Throughout the firm's long history in Idaho, it has proudly maintained the tradition of civic involvement and public service launched over 100 years ago by James Hawley.

Contributing to the communities in which they work and live is important to the people of Hawley Troxell. Volunteering on projects such as Habitat for Humanity's "First Ladies Build" and City Light Home for Women and Children enables the employees to help make a difference in their community.

The driving force behind the firm's commitment is its desire to strengthen its communities. In addition to the helping hands of its volunteers, employees are active members and serve in leadership positions of various civic organizations.

As the state's largest and oldest law firm, Hawley Troxell is very effective in recruiting legal talent.

With a growing number of clients throughout the western United States, the firm provides services beyond the boundaries of the Gem State and represents its clients' national and international interests.

Hawley Troxell has never been a firm content to rest on its history and reputation. It is a business-oriented firm providing representation and assistance in business transactions and litigation services, with nearly one-half of the practice in litigation. The company provides a wide range of services for personal and business legal needs, representing clients before all state and federal courts and administrative agencies.

Hawley Troxell delivers a vast array of services efficiently and economically with the help of technology. A commitment to maintain the pace with advancements in the practice of law helps members of the firm to conduct sophisticated informational analysis, document retrieval and exchange, and litigation management. Computerized research capabilities combine with one of the state's largest private law libraries to give the company's attorneys an additional advantage.

With over 100 years experience in law, Hawley Troxell continues to build on the high standards of its founders and the proud tradition of its name with a commitment to serving the needs and goals of its clients.

habitec

ARCHITECTURE ■ PLANNING ■ INTERIOR DESIGN

In 1972 three architects in the San Francisco Bay Area started a collaboration that combined the disciplines of architecture, land planning, and interior design, along with a hands-on understanding of construction. Their focus was to see quality developments with people-friendly spaces constructed at a reasonable cost in the Silicon Valley. The name given to the firm was Habitec and its extensive portfolio is evident with over 25 million square feet of constructed building area, over 10 million square feet of interior space designed, and over 2,500 acres of business park development.

While the office located in San Jose continued to flourish, Habitec recognized an opportunity to establish a presence in the Boise area and serve clients in the Treasure Valley, greater Idaho, and the northwestern states. Therefore, in 1994, Habitec opened its second office in Boise. The office moved to Eagle, Idaho in 2000 and presently has a staff of six. While each office operates independently, both are available to offer staffing, as well as technical support, to the other.

Habitec's areas of expertise are extensive in scope and range. The firm has been instrumental in the successful development of many business parks, multi-tenant buildings, manufacturing, industrial, educational and recreational facilities, and various retail and commercial properties. It has also designed office buildings, warehouses, restaurants, laboratories, and residential projects in its 30 years of existence. Currently, the firm's architects are NCARB certified and are registered to practice architecture in eight states.

Habitec advocates the design-build process, a project delivery system that performs both design and construction under one contract. The benefits of this process include one point of contact and responsibility for the work involved as well as tighter cost control. The firm also specializes in the design of buildings using concrete "tilt-up" construction technology, producing innovative and unique design solutions. Design possibilities for tilt-up construction are as limitless and varied as the architect's imagination.

Rivershore North Lobby, Eagle, Idaho.

The success of Habitec can be traced to its ability in providing creative solutions for each of its clients. In addition to creativity, these solutions recognize project practicality, user functionality, and realistic budget and timeline constraints. Keeping clients satisfied by being responsive to their needs through all phases of the project is also a very important factor behind Habitec's success. From the initial planning and design stages to cost management and through construction, Habitec stays in touch with the client and follows through on all phases of the project, giving the client a peace of mind that many other firms may not be able to sustain. And it's that type of service and genuine care for each client that has solidified the company's reputation as a leader in its field. ■

Rivershore North, Eagle, Idaho.

Photo © David R. Frazier Photolibrary

9

Real Estate, Development, & Construction

Steed Construction, 128

Thornton Oliver Keller, 132

John L. Scott Real Estate, 134

Petra, 136

F&C Corporation and Rocky Mountain Management & Development, LLC, 138

CM Company, Inc., 139

Photo © David R. Frazier Photolibrary

Steed Construction

When it comes time to build a new building, many business owners and developers turn to Steed Construction for its ability to act as a creative one-stop shop handling all of their needs in a complete and efficient manner.

Steed Construction is a general contractor that has become one of the most successful and fastest-growing companies in Idaho, specializing in design/build commercial and light industrial construction projects throughout the western United States. Its success lies in the fact that the principals are trusted individuals, shouldering a strong reputation for meeting each commitment that they assume and providing quality projects with creative and flexible solutions at a competitive price. This is done while maintaining a high level of integrity as well as an excellent work environment with genuine and equal concern for both their clients and employees.

Ram International selected Steed Construction to demolish and re-build their Murphy's Restaurant on Broadway in Boise. The hospitality industry has become an ever-increasing part of Steed Construction's business including hotel and food service construction.

The Eagle Market Place Shopping Center, designed by BRS Architects is an example of the many suburban retail centers that Steed Construction has built throughout the Treasure Valley.

After nearly 20 years of working in the construction industry, serving as a project manager and vice president of two high-profile construction firms in the San Jose, California area, Randy Steed founded Steed Construction, Inc. in 1988. Randy was contacted by a former co-worker of his, Scott Raymes about the possibility of them opening a second office in the Boise area where Scott had moved his family in 1984 to seek a better life style. Randy visited the Boise area and fell in love with the beauty, the way of life, and the business potential that the area had to offer. Randy and Scott became equal partners and opened a second office of Steed Construction in the Boise area in 1993. Randy also followed Scotts' lead and moved his family to the area. In 1994, the Boise office

This farm building design by ZGA Architects is one of two built by Steed in the North Channel Business Park in Eagle where Steed has constructed the five anchor buildings for their clients Baker & Brandt.

Tenant Improvements varying from high tech to retail continue to be a mainstay for Steed Construction as illustrated by this tenant improvement for CRI Advantage located in Park Pointe Center II.

ITT's 30,000-square-foot facility located in Boise Research Park is an example of the fast track design/build process. The facility was designed, permitted, and constructed in only a few weeks to meet their client's tight time schedule.

became the principal office and by 1995, the team decided to close the Bay Area office and devote all their energies to the Boise office.

Today, Steed Construction is licensed to operate in 11 western states from Texas to Washington and has built more than 180 structures in that area. The variety of buildings that Steed has constructed spans the gamut and includes commercial and industrial buildings and interiors for offices, warehouse/distribution, retail, call centers, advanced technology, education, manufacturing, telecommunications, medical/dental, hospitality, and restaurants. Between Randy Steed and Scott Raymes, the two have overseen projects that are a virtual "Who's Who" of name brand corporations such as IBM, EDS, FMC, Atari, Apple Computers, ITT, Lockheed, Con Agra, Agilent, Adaptec, GTE, CRI Advantage, In-systems, Hewlett Packard, Sprint PCS, Cricket Communications, Electric Lightwave, Albertson's, and AT&T Wireless.

The company is well known for being one of the most progressive, reputable contractors in the state of Idaho, specializing in commercial and industrial buildings, as well as innovative tilt-up structures. Steed Construction has earned a reputation for being one of the more creative firms in their area of business.

"We've gathered extensive experience over the years from both the Bay Area and here," Randy says. "We have some close strategic alliances with customers, architects, and subcontractors which allows us to put projects together that other firms aren't able to match. We're able to solve problems before they occur and are fortunate enough to be able to develop creative solutions to challenges in each project that we undertake."

One of the more unique commitments at Steed Construction is its team approach to design and construction. By creating a team atmosphere amongst its employees, the potential for a volatile work environment is minimized and a productive group that works together to achieve company goals on a daily basis is formed. The people at Steed Construction firmly believe that the key to successful project management is for everyone to pull together in the early stages of planning and follow through to the project's culmination.

Most of Steed Construction's business is generated through word of mouth and repeat clients. The majority of its customers appreciate the one-stop shop service that they receive at Steed,

The Rivershore North and South Office Buildings designed by Habitec total 64,000 square feet and are a beautiful example of the more than 50 office buildings that Steed Construction has built throughout Idaho.

Steed Construction was selected by J.C. Penny Co. to completely remodel their 150,274-square-foot department store located at the Boise Towne Square Mall. The project was completed in 37 phases while the store remained open and operational.

This Knox facility at Fiberpipe's facility in the Emerald Tech Park is an example of the many telecommunication and switch facilities that Steed has constructed throughout the Northwest for customers such as AT&T Wireless, Sprint PCS, Cellular One, Electric Lightwave, and Cricket Communications.

where the design, budgeting, bidding, negotiating, and construction are all managed by one company with one point of responsibility, encompassing every minute detail that goes into the construction of each project. "We try to make our structure easy for our clients," says Randy. "Some of our competitors seem to make the process that their clients are about to go through difficult to understand. We try to put their mind at ease and carefully explain what we are going to do in an easy and painless way, creating a high level of trust and a lot less headaches for our customers. We handle everything throughout the process from the design to the various problems that creep up unexpectedly. We keep the communications open and make the entire process as easy and carefree for the customer as we possibly can. Most importantly, we are able to show and tell our customers what their finished product will look like and what it will cost without them having to spend a significant amount of money beforehand. Those are the advantages to having a one-stop design/build shop."

Being one of the more successful contractors in the area has afforded Steed Construction the opportunity to give back to the community in ways that many businesses could not. Alongside the usual donations and advertising with non-profit, charitable, and school groups, Steed Construction has been fortunate to be in the position to do other things such as build a skateboard park for the city of Eagle so that the city's youth have a place to play other than on the city's sidewalks. They obtained donations and oversaw the construction of a press box for Centennial High School's football field when the school found itself unable to raise the funds for the expensive amenity.

Local developers Kowallis and Mackey selected Steed Construction to design and build a new 109,248-square-foot mixed-use project in Jackson Hole, Wyoming. The project includes two levels of parking, retail on the first level, and 44 condominiums on the second and third floors. The project is scheduled to be complete in September of 2002.

"We get a fair amount of people asking us for assistance," Scott says. 'We try to help out whenever we can. Both Randy and I have children in school and we realize what good can come out of our company's involvement when we become involved with projects that help the community."

Steed Construction plans to both expand and diversify the business in the coming years. As Idaho continues to mature as a principal market, Steed Construction is hopeful that it too will continue to grow with the marketplace. New challenges such as parking structures and mid- and high-rise buildings are presenting

Western Power Sports selected Steed Construction and Habitec Architects to design and construct the 108,000-square-foot first phase of their new corporate headquarter/distribution facility located off Gowen Road in Boise. Eventually the facility will expand to over 400,000 square feet on 32 acres.

The Old Navy and related shops at the Family Center in Meridian are an example of the "Big Box" retail facilities that Steed Construction has had the privilege of constructing for a variety of clients throughout the Northwest.

unique opportunities for the company to use its past experience to expand its horizons and tackle larger projects.

"I see us doing more mixed-use projects and probably more work in the healthcare and extended-care areas as the population ages," Randy said. "Hospitality also seems to be a growing part of our market in such facilities as hotels and restaurants. We expect to expand our services outside the radius that we're currently in and continue to work in a wider range of states. We're not actively seeking work out of state, but we have had customers that we have worked with in the past who are expanding into different markets and have asked us to help them expand their marketplace. So we seem to be growing quite well in that respect." Scott said.

Randy and Scott were able to sum up their company's success in one quick anecdote. "A few years ago, we asked a customer of ours why he continued to use and recommend us. He told us, it's because you do what you say you are going to do when you say you are going to do it. What a concept."

It is a simple statement really, " Randy says. "But it is an amazing concept to build a successful business around." ■

Steed Construction has teamed up with several of the areas leading architects to design and build a wide variety of projects as illustrated by this preliminary design for a new parking structure to be located in downtown Boise. Steed's design partner for this project is CSHQA of Boise.

Thornton Oliver Keller

What a difference a decade makes. Just ten short years ago, Thornton Oliver Keller opened its doors as a commercial real estate company with an innovative vision for the local commercial real estate industry and the impact it could have on the Boise market. Hard work, coupled with a professional delivery of services and a determination to exceed the expectations of each and every client, have proven to be a successful formula for the firm, which has grown in size from two employees in 1991 to over 90 full time professionals in 2002. To its credit, Thornton Oliver Keller hasn't allowed its commitment to excellent service to be sacrificed by this explosive growth. In fact, the Boise Metro Chamber of Commerce named Thornton Oliver Keller the 1999 small business of the year in the "medium" sized business category.

Since its inception, the firm has been unique in its service, specialization, and selection, offering clients comprehensive commercial real estate brokerage and property management services. What does that mean for the businesses' every day activities? Simply put, Thornton Oliver Keller offers unmatched professional services to their clients. The firm's real estate experts specialize in all aspects of commercial real estate brokerage. Industrial, office, retail, and investment product representation are all well within their core capabilities. Thornton Oliver Keller represents the interests of many national companies and major Boise businesses. Among others, Thornton Oliver Keller represents (or has represented) US West (Qwest), USF Reddaway, International Paper, Starbucks, Amresco, IBM, Albertson's, American Express, Office Depot, RiteAid, 24 Hour Fitness, Schucks Auto Supply, Xpedx, Postal Annex, Great Clips, Pep Boys, Roundtable Pizza, Red Lobster, Costco, and Washington Group (formerly Morrison Knudsen Corporation), to name a few.

Thornton Oliver Keller has differentiated itself from its competitors by integrating their real estate expertise, broad market

presence, and powerful new technologies, which offers each client a systematic method for evaluating their commercial real estate options and goals.

Thornton Oliver Keller continues to represent some of the most cutting edge development projects in Boise. For example, the firm has been the exclusive marketing agent for the Boise Research Center since 1992.

The firm's approach to business has always been centered upon a promise to "represent properties that are well located, well designed, and well built," according to Peter Oliver.

Taking the long-range view of the community is at the heart of Thornton Oliver Keller's business practices. As Boise continues to grow, Thornton Oliver Keller will work to keep it an attractive, pleasant community. Everyone at Thornton Oliver Keller works hard to be a vital part of this valley by giving back in meaningful ways.

As the business has grown, Thornton Oliver Keller has emerged as the local leader in property management, asset management, leasing, and sales services for the sophisticated individual and/or corporate real estate investor.

Complementing the firm's brokerage services, are Thornton Oliver Keller's property management services. Thornton Oliver Keller utilizes a hands-on approach in management relations with each owner, advisor, venture partner, and tenant, thereby ensuring effective communication and the realization of client objectives.

Thornton Oliver Keller's current commercial property management portfolio is in excess of 3.5 million square feet. The multifamily management division of the company boasts approximately 1,037 multifamily units, more than any other commercial management firm in the state.

How does Thornton Oliver Keller meet its clients' ever changing property management needs? It conducts exhaustive surveys and analyzes all tenant contact through a scheduled management program, which offers the client the opportunity to continually update and restructure its procedures.

The firm's goal is to maximize each property's utility and, therefore, tenancy. Thornton Oliver Keller's portfolio provides a diverse inventory of space, which offers property managers the ability to manage each owner's property with skill and expertise gained from both past and present management experiences.

Thornton Oliver Keller firmly believes that its success is a direct result of its employees' hard work. With that in mind, the firm's management team recently completed a project that laid out the company's blueprint for the future, defining corporate vision, mission, purpose, and strategies. At the heart of the company is its purpose: "To serve people."

The company places high value on teamwork, results, ideas, fun, communication, freedom, integrity, customer service and satisfaction, a quality market presence, compassion, respect, commitment, adaptability, and an equipped workforce. Thornton Oliver Keller is unique because of the leadership exhibited by partners Tim Thornton, Peter Oliver, and Mike Keller. Refusing to micro-manage any of their employees, they provide the staff with an infrastructure and culture that is always willing to supply information, guidance, or any tools needed to do the job at hand. The partners lead by example, demonstrating the highest degree of ethics, excellent work habits, a commendable appreciation for family life, and a love of their jobs.

They are enthusiasts, intent on building an industrial-strength creative company. The company will continue to grow, in part, by staying true to its mission, which is to "Weave together the most capable and highly trained, motivated people in an environment of innovation, information, and teamwork to dominate the markets we serve."

John L. Scott Real Estate

For over 70 years, John L. Scott Real Estate has been in the business of assisting people in making a smooth transition from one home to another. Today, the company stands proud as the largest independent residential real estate company in the Northwest with over 2,800 sales associates in more than 100 offices throughout Washington, Oregon, and Idaho. And it still manages to uphold the values and principles that the company was founded upon in 1931.

Locally, John L. Scott Boise has been in the real estate business since 1984, becoming the fourth corner in the company's square of locations, the other three being in Seattle, Portland, and Spokane. The company has gone to great lengths to remain instrumental in creating a new standard of service for clients, associates, and employees in the real estate industry, providing a one-stop information center for all of its clients' real estate buying and selling needs. The company has always provided its clients with the best full service in the industry, doing what serves its clients best even if it doesn't fit into the traditional method of doing business. This is accomplished by being honest and realistic with each of its clients, never overpricing properties, or representing buyers who are unrealistic about the conditions of homes. The agents and management of John L. Scott Real Estate are all highly motivated, honest, ethical, goal-oriented, and forward thinking, and are consistently seeking out better ways in which to conduct business by taking chances and entertaining new ideas for the industry. By staying true to those traits, the company helps achieve its overall goal of being the most professional, productive, and positive real estate office in the United States.

With a commitment to quality in every action it performs, John L. Scott Real Estate has emerged as a leader in the industry

John L. Scott Real Estate Boise office located in West Boise at the Boise Research Center.

within the Treasure Valley. Employing over 150 agents and 20 office employees, John L. Scott Boise features specialists in areas of tax-deferred exchanges, new home community marketing, land acquisition, and the resale of clients' existing homes. The company is also well skilled in commercial leasing activities, being behind the sales of all types of businesses, ranging from duplexes to multi-million dollar commercial centers. The dedication provided by each of the company's agents and employees has paid off as John L. Scott Real Estate has become the ninth most productive real estate company in the nation as far as unit and volume count.

Over the last 20 years, the accessibility of information and knowledge to the consumer has required a different level of service from the real estate associate and broker. With the onslaught of the Internet and its massive popularity, it has become crucial that the real estate industry be well represented in cyberspace. While in the

Craig Groves, President/owner, and Bob Bass, Principal Broker/owner, are committed to creating a new standard of service for clients, associates, and employees in the real estate industry.

The John L. Scott Foundation strives to give back to the community through its commitment to children and their medical needs.

Believing in the community and the benefits that the community can provide a business, John L. Scott Real Estate created the John L. Scott Foundation, a foundation funded by the generous donations and volunteer efforts of the John L.Scott sales associates and employees. Utilizing voluntary contributions from agents and staff members, the Foundation has been able to make contributions to the Saint Luke's Children's Hospital for several years, ensuring that all children in Boise have access to medical care regardless of their family's financial status. By giving back to the community in that way, the community has given back to the company by making it one of the most successful real estate companies in the entire industry.

past, consumers had no choice but to go to the real estate agent or broker for information on real estate, today all of that information is available online. John L. Scott Real Estate was the first company in the nation to develop an Internet home page for every property that is listed and sold by the company. The company's Web site (www.johnlscott.com) has been cited as one of the best marketing sites in the country in terms of ease of use in discovering each of the company's listings. The Web site has been such a success for the company that it won the coveted Innovative Service Award for its Internet Property Link and has been cited as one of the first real estate brokers to push broker reciprocity, allowing every real estate broker in the country the opportunity to view each other's listings and share electronic data. Today, all listings offered by John L. Scott are available on a variety of popular real estate Web sites including realtor.com and the Microsoft Home Advisor.

The success of John L. Scott Boise has led to the establishment of the organization's Relocation Services Company. Formed in 1987, the Relocation Services Company assists clients in the transition into and out of their homes, helping everyone from executives to interns. The three full-time staff members assist clients one-on-one, providing tours of the new areas while orientating the clients on their new neighborhood and fielding whatever questions the client may have about their new home and community.

The company's Web site (www.johnlscott.com) has been cited as one of the best marketing sites in the country.

Petra

"Rock Solid." That phrase is emblazoned in the work of the people at Petra Incorporated, one of Boise's premier general contractors. For nearly a decade, Petra has devoted itself to building a rock solid team that takes pride in offering rock solid service. The Petra team has more than 75 years of combined experience in project management, and specializes in the personal service required to fulfill each client's construction needs. The secret to their team spirit is providing a rock solid foundation for every client and every facility.

After working in the commercial construction industry for more than 20 years, owner Jerry Frank fulfilled his dream of starting his own construction firm. Since 1994, Jerry has worked hard to build a motivated team that creates satisfied clients by offering quality construction with precise attention to the details of a project and doing it with excellent customer service. Jerry's construction experiences, along with his standards for service, have created a solid foundation for Petra Incorporated that will last for many generations.

Offering broad yet specialized experience in the commercial construction industry, Petra takes pride in catering its services to meet every client's construction needs. Concrete tilt-up, poured in place concrete structures, steel and glass, masonry, E.I.F.S., and conventional wood structures are some of the many types of buildings within Petra's experience. Through these projects, Petra has developed into a leader in the construction industry in Idaho and extending throughout the Pacific Northwest.

Petra has always made an effort to undertake a wide variety of projects for a diverse clientele. Petra was the contractor of choice for Boise Towne Plaza because of the company's strong reputation and competitive pricing.

Petra also had great success in building the Blackeagle and South Cole Business Centers in Boise. Both are shining examples of quality workmanship. More construction success stories came after the completion of medical-related projects for the Boise Endoscopy Center

Idaho Athletic Club, a 45,000-square-foot full-service club. *Photo by Phil McClain*

and Saint Luke's Regional Medical Center. Both clients benefited from Petra's commitment to detail and client satisfaction.

In addition, Petra has experience in constructing multi-building complexes and infrastructures, dental complexes, worship centers, educational facilities, office/flex buildings, motels, apartment complexes, housing units, food manufacturing facilities, company call centers, manufacturing plants, and much more.

At Petra, the office staff and field personnel have made the commitment to build projects of superior quality by serving the needs of each client with integrity and cost effectiveness.

"Building relationships one building at a time" is another phrase associated with Petra. The company estimates nearly 80 percent of its commissioned work is negotiated. Petra works through repeat clients and their referrals to build a rock solid clientele. Repeat business has helped develop trusted relationships between each client and the Petra team. The Petra team has set the goal to grow

Northwest Lodge, a 69-room hotel with suites and conference facilities. *Photo by Phil McClain*

into one of the top general contractors in the Treasure Valley. The team is on course to meet that goal.

Petra is "A Rock in the Community" through its involvement in the Drug Free Idaho Program and other community service organizations. Jerry Frank was asked to serve as the President of the Drug Free Idaho Program because of his commitment to improve the construction industry's growing challenge of drugs in the workplace. The program requires mandatory drug testing for all employees. In an effort to improve public perception of construction field workers, he implemented the stringent program at Petra's business office and on every job site. The Petra team enthusiastically supports and promotes the program.

Jerry has found the Drug Free Idaho Program offers his team a healthier working environment and provides the reward of safer, more accident free job sites. Jerry believes the Drug Free Idaho Program is good for businesses, employees, and the community.

Petra successfully builds relationships with clients and the community. The Petra team understands the importance of excellence in customer care, integrity, and accountability to owners, developers, and subcontractors. Petra is committed to building long-term relationships because Petra is committed to being part of the community for many years to come.

Petra-**Rock Solid** in the construction industry, in its commitment to excellence, in the community.

St. Luke's Meridian, a full-service hospital addition. *Photo by Phil McClain*

Blackeagle Business Center, a 40-acre business park with office/flex buildings and retail buildings. Construction of new retail space is planned for the open parcel in the center of photo. *Photo by Phil McClain*

"We understand how important it is to treat our clients with honesty, integrity, and excellent service so they never feel the need to look elsewhere for a contractor to meet their construction needs."

Jerry Frank, Owner

F&C Corporation and Rocky Mountain Management & Development, LLC

As the business market in Boise continues to expand dramatically, there is a continued necessity for available office space in the area. The F & C Corporation and it's group of related companies has stepped to the forefront of the real estate business, owning, operating, and developing not only commercial real estate properties serving several businesses in the city, but also hotels throughout Idaho, Montana, Washington, and Oregon. It's sister company, Rocky Mountain Management & Development, handles the administrative and development work for all of the different entities resulting in a successful marriage of the two companies to form a powerful force in the local commercial real estate industry. The company owns and manages just under 280,000 square feet of office and flex buildings. Four of those buildings are in the Portland area, while the other ten commercial buildings are located here in the Treasure Valley.

Founded in Boise in 1978, F & C and Rocky Mountain Management & Development has created several hundred jobs over the years in the construction of its properties in the city as well as the ongoing operations of the company's managed motels. Combined, they keep approximately 150 local residents employed in the Treasure Valley. It is the ownership, operation, and development of these motels that sets F & C Corporation and Rocky Mountain Management & Development apart from its competition. With the ability to develop and manage both hotels and office space, F & C is able to provide more diversification for its investors and clients.

F & C Corporation and Rocky Mountain Management & Development intends to continue growing both sides of its business

Airport Business Park.

as well as provide development services for others. Because the company provides its own development, management, and leasing of its properties, there has been an increase in inquiries from professionals who would like that same service for their buildings. Thus, there's an opportunity to expand the company by providing its expertise in development services to other professionals. The company is also looking to expand in the Northwest.

Above all, the main reason companies turn to F & C Corporation and Rocky Mountain Management & Development is for its integrity in conducting business. The corporation has repeatedly been nominated for the Better Business Bureau's Integrity Counts Award, based strictly upon its honest and open approach in dealing with its clients. Because at F & C Corporation and Rocky Mountain Management & Development, they believe that business should be conducted fairly and in a manner in which its customers should expect to be treated. It may be one of the oldest rules in doing business, but it's a rule that has made the corporation the success that it has become. ■

F&C Corporation's Corporate Office.

CM Company, Inc.

Since 1977, CM Company has provided construction management and general contracting services for more than a third of a billion dollars worth of commercial building projects in both the public and private sectors. The craftsmanship of CM Company is evident in some of the Treasure Valley's most impressive structures, including the 11-story Washington Mutual Capitol Plaza, Meridian's new Mountain View High School, Portland's 258-suite River Place Residence Inn Hotel, and the renovation of the 100 year-old Boise High School. However, according to partners Dennis Robinson and Ray Hoobing, the first and most important thing CM Company builds into each job doesn't have anything to do with steel or concrete. CM Company is dedicated to building a customer's trust.

"That may sound simplistic," Robinson explained. "Yet it's the truth. We've worked hard to develop a reputation of being a company that can be trusted—trusted to build a quality building, trusted to deal with the customer in an ethical manner, trusted to provide cutting edge management techniques, and trusted to meet an owner's expectations."

No other aspect of CM Company speaks to its success quite as powerfully as its people. Idaho natives, Robinson and Hoobing have architectural backgrounds and possess strong experience as project managers and estimators. Since founding the company, Dennis and Ray continue building a team of employees with experience and backgrounds, which enhance the company's ability to meet its clients' needs.

Long before construction begins, CM Company personnel join with the owner and designers to form a strong design/construction team that can develop a building design that meets the owner's aesthetic, functional, and economical requirements. As a design is developed, CM Company's staff prepares progressively more

Washington Mutual Capitol Plaza—Mixed Used Building.

detailed project budgets, provides constructability review, develops a construction schedule, and finally produces a guaranteed cost.

Meeting an owner's schedule and effectively managing the on-site construction is critical for construction success. To effectively control their projects, CM Company project managers produce a critical path network schedule that identifies all the required activities, their durations, and sequence for completion. This schedule becomes the "Bible" around which the project manager and managing superintendent direct all construction activities.

CM Company is set apart from its competitors by the years of accumulated construction experience, which enables CM's staff to more effectively use state-of-the-art management tools. CM Company's systems, architectural knowledge, and its staff's efforts to understand an owner's business combine to help CM Company personnel "look beyond the blueprints," and to anticipate construction challenges before they become construction problems.

Finally, even after the construction crews have left the job and an owner has moved in, CM personnel continue working with an owner to ensure his continued satisfaction with the finished product. It's all part of a commitment to integrity and the pursuit of trust.

River Quarry Office Buildings.

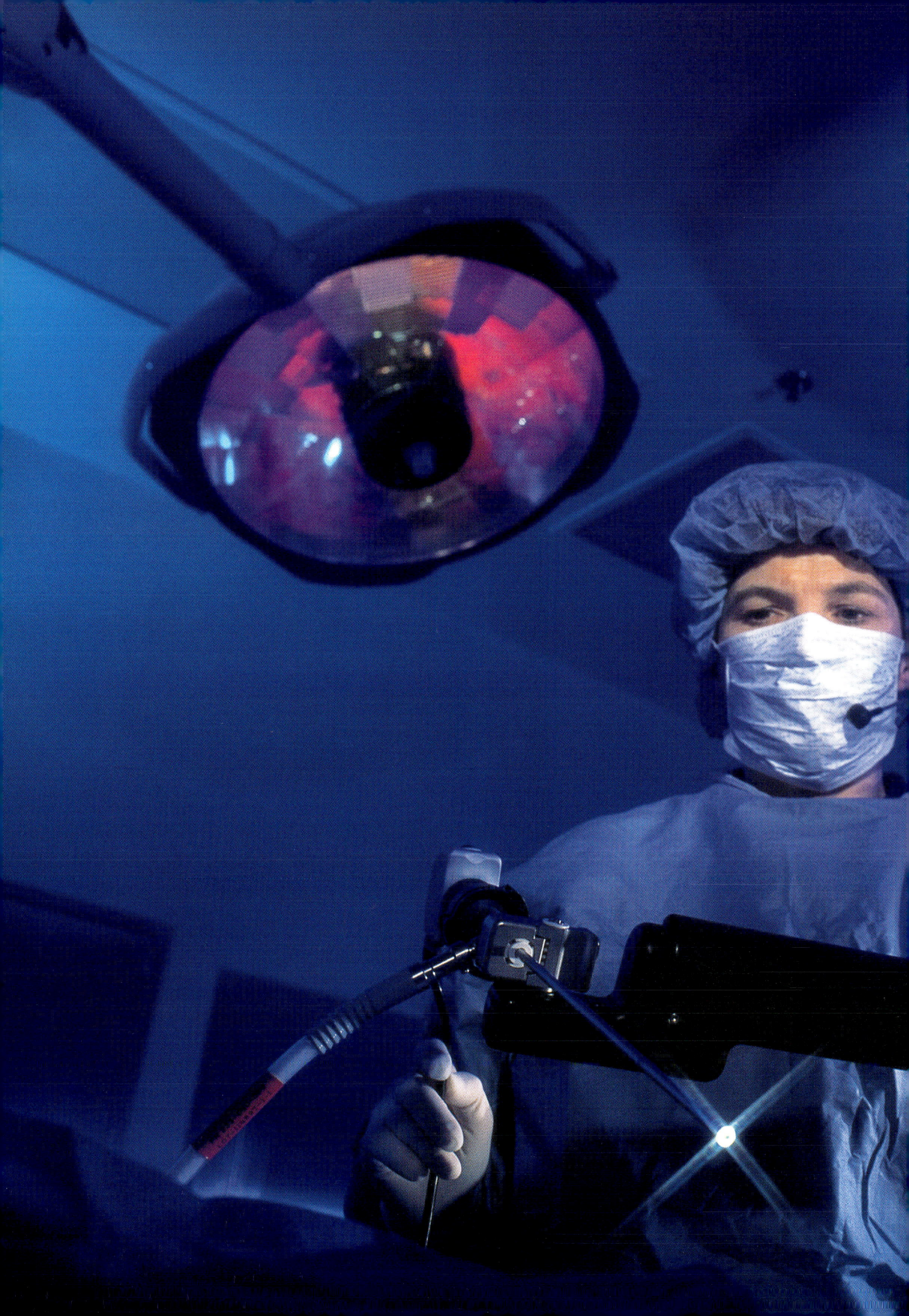

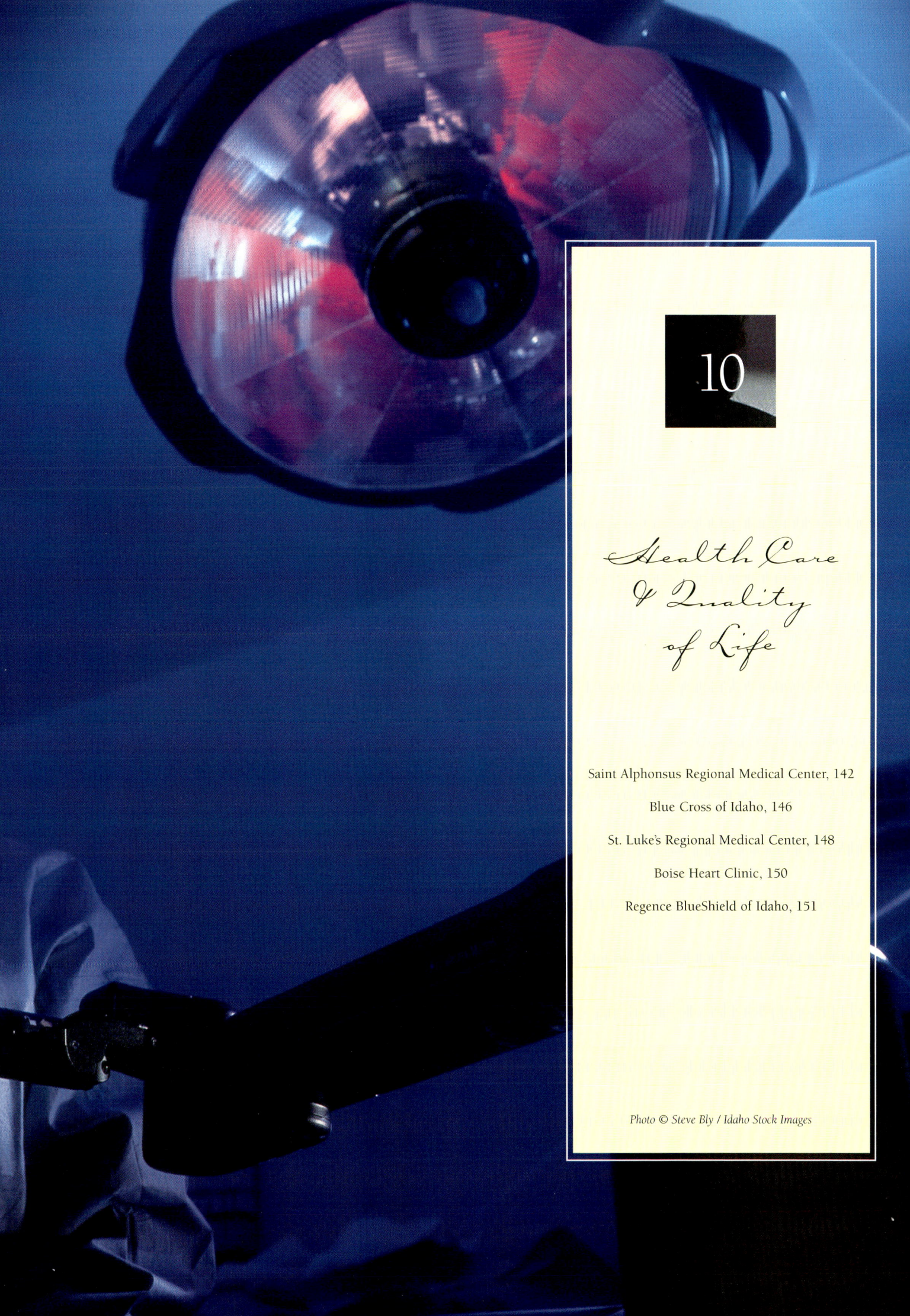

10

Health Care & Quality of Life

Saint Alphonsus Regional Medical Center, 142

Blue Cross of Idaho, 146

St. Luke's Regional Medical Center, 148

Boise Heart Clinic, 150

Regence BlueShield of Idaho, 151

Photo © Steve Bly / Idaho Stock Images

Saint Alphonsus Regional Medical Center

Delivering advanced healing and medical "firsts" to the community

Through skilled staff and state-of-the-art technologies, Saint Alphonsus Regional Medical Center delivers advanced healing services throughout southwest Idaho, eastern Oregon and northern Nevada. Established in downtown Boise in 1894 by the Sisters of the Holy Cross Catholic order, Saint Alphonsus has served the region for over a century in the sprit of a faith-based mission. In the beginning, four Sisters served as nurses, bringing healthcare to the poor and underserved, a mission that remains intact today. In 1972, the hospital made a bold move, relocating from downtown to its current location on Curtis Road. Once a vacant dirt lot filled with sagebrush, the site now serves as the center for advanced medicine that is poised to support the community well into the future.

Leadership and innovation take a vast array of clinical expertise, dedication, and commitment. Saint Alphonsus has fulfilled this role, receiving ongoing recognition to underline this point. The hospital established the first and only ACS Level II Trauma Center in Idaho, providing immediate critical care to patients in a 100,000-square-mile region.

In support of its critical care center, Saint Alphonsus Life Flight has provided the area with over 16 years of safe medical air transport service. The state's first nationally accredited air ambulance service, Saint Alphonsus Life Flight contains advanced life-saving equipment—including devices for critically ill newborns. Operating from three bases with a fleet of three helicopters and a fixed-wing airplane, the team of specially trained flight nurses, paramedics, and emergency medical technicians has flown over 15,000 missions and serves parts of Oregon, Nevada, and Washington, as well as southern Idaho.

Saint Alphonsus attracts and retains among the best and brightest healthcare practitioners in the region. Physicians and clinical

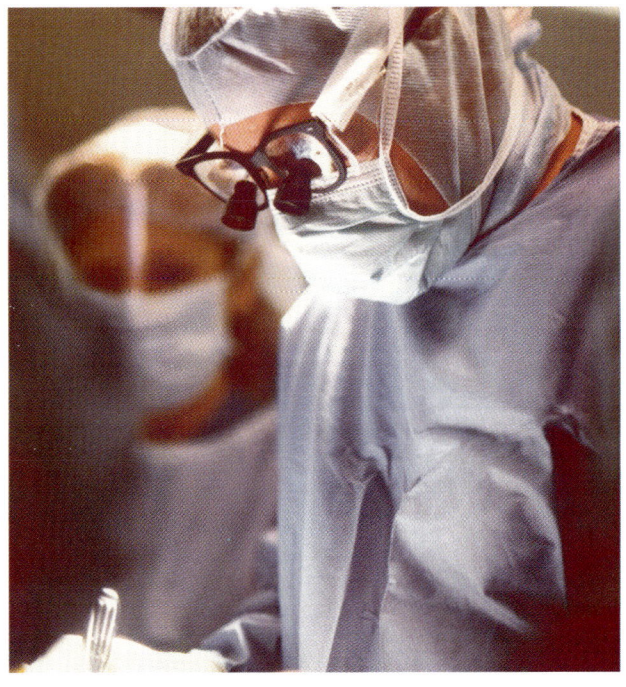

Saint Alphonsus has been a community leader in innovative, quality healthcare for over one hundred years.

professionals at 18 affiliated clinics throughout the Treasure Valley support Saint Alphonsus, providing easy access to local medical expertise and assuring a higher level of quality healthcare.

As far back as 1900 when the hospital installed the first X-ray equipment in Idaho, Saint Alphonsus has been known for innovation in technology and treatment. Their radiology team is comprised of renowned physicians in a community-based setting, utilizing protocols, research, and experience gained from nationally ranked medical schools and affiliated hospitals.

A view of the north and south towers of the Curtis Road campus at dusk.

Gardens in the Family Maternity Center offer families a relaxing environment to get to know their newest addition.

To complement this team of diagnostic and interventional specialists, Saint Alphonsus houses leading edge medical imaging technology, including multi-slice computed tomography (CT) and positron emission tomography (PET) scanners, providing non-invasive diagnosis options for patients in and around Boise.

Saint Alphonsus also established one of the first Picture Archiving Communication Systems (PACS) in the state. This system replaces traditional X-ray film with digitally produced images that transfer along Intranet and Internet systems, improving speed, access, and viewing methods essential for diagnosis. In recognition of its technical advancements, Saint Alphonsus has consistently received the "Top 100 Most Wired" hospitals in the nation award.

To complement traditional surgery techniques, Saint Alphonsus invested in a robotic surgical platform, used to perform minimally invasive procedures that result in shorter hospital stays, less surgical risks, and faster recovery periods. A central part of the "operating room of the future," these robotic assistants are vastly improving patient outcomes and surgical efforts.

In 2001, the hospital adopted Idaho's first Transfusion-Free Medicine and Surgery program. This program meets the needs of patients who are compelled by religious or safety reasons to avoid blood transfusions, relying on their own recycled blood or surgical blood-sparing procedures.

The same year, Saint Alphonsus expanded and improved its Family Maternity Center, illustrating its commitment to the community's families. A Level III Neonatal Intensive Care Unit was added, supported by the top neonatal physicians in the area who established the primary protocols of care for the community's tiniest patients. The Family Maternity Center has a unique labor, delivery, and recovery model, where new mothers and their families experience the delight of childbirth in one convenient location—a private, comfortable birth suite. Saint Alphonsus is also the first certified Lamaze Approved Provider in the area, an acknowledgement of its standard of excellence in childbirth preparation classes.

An exclusive and "first" provider of neurological services, Saint Alphonsus is home to the only neurological center in the state. The Idaho Neurological Institute (INI) was recently ranked 11th in the country for the number of patients treated and fourth in the country for care of actual spinal cases. INI Innovations include minimally invasive procedures aimed at improving patient outcomes as well as consumer education programs regarding strokes, head trauma, and injury prevention.

In the fall of 2001, an INI neurosurgeon teamed up with an interventional radiologist to perform the first Gugleilmi Detachable Coil (GDC) procedure in the community. This advanced procedure enhances the physician's ability to treat patients who are high risk for traditional brain aneurysm surgery. Along with technologically advanced services, the INI at Saint Alphonsus provides a continuum of care. This continuum includes acute care and rehabilitation services designed to reintegrate individuals into a pre-injury lifestyle, including employment, community, and recreational activities.

Recognized among the "Top 100 Hospitals" in the nation for cardiovascular care, the Saint Alphonsus Heart Center, in conjunction with top cardiologists and cardiovascular surgeons in the community, continuously provides superior cardiac care utilizing the latest medical equipment.

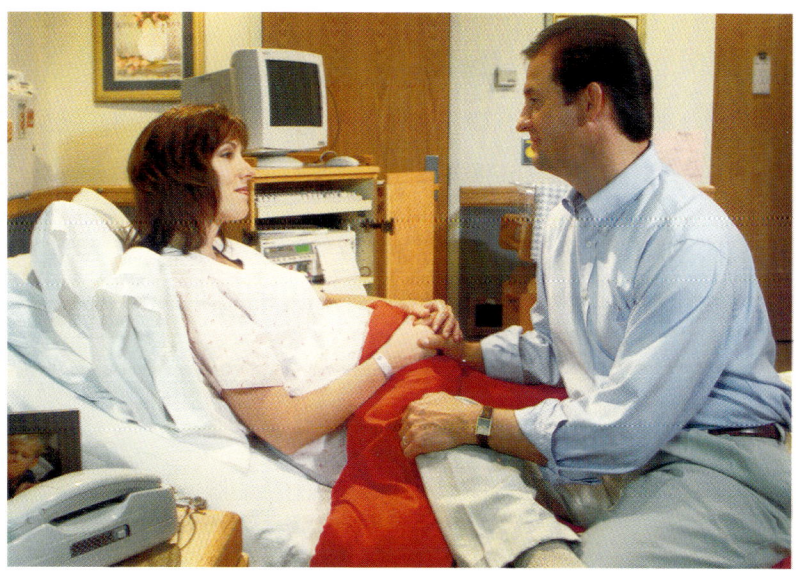

Private, spacious suites allow mothers to experience childbirth-labor, deliver, and recover all in one room, with the baby never leaving the mother's side.

Tele-cardiology capabilities and a renovated Endovascular Suite are examples of such cardiac advancements. With tele-cardiology, medical staff can view side-by-side images of the heart wall and associated motion and flow, transmitted via fiber optic lines, eliminating wait time and allowing for immediate advice and diagnosis. The Endovascular Suite is considered one of the most unique in the nation, utilizing an advanced technology that enables three-dimensional image reconstruction of the circulatory system for more precise treatment. The lab, using a care system of cardiologists, vascular surgeons, and interventional radiologists, provides a collaborative, multi-disciplined approach that streamlines the diagnosis and treatment process for patients with vascular disease.

For cancer patients, the Saint Alphonsus Cancer Treatment Center has developed an exceptional, holistic approach to treating patients that addresses their physical, emotional, and spiritual needs. This care integrates proven complementary therapies, such as nutrition, yoga, stress reduction and pain management techniques, with conventional medical treatments to enhance recovery and quality of life for patients. In 2000, through a partnership with West Valley Medical Center, Saint Alphonsus expanded cancer care in the Treasure Valley with the opening of a 9,000-square-foot cancer treatment center in Caldwell that integrates personal cancer care services with state-of-the-art technology for treating tumors.

As a continuation of its original commitment to the community, Saint Alphonsus provided nearly $27 million in charity care in 2001. In addition to its generous charitable contributions to the

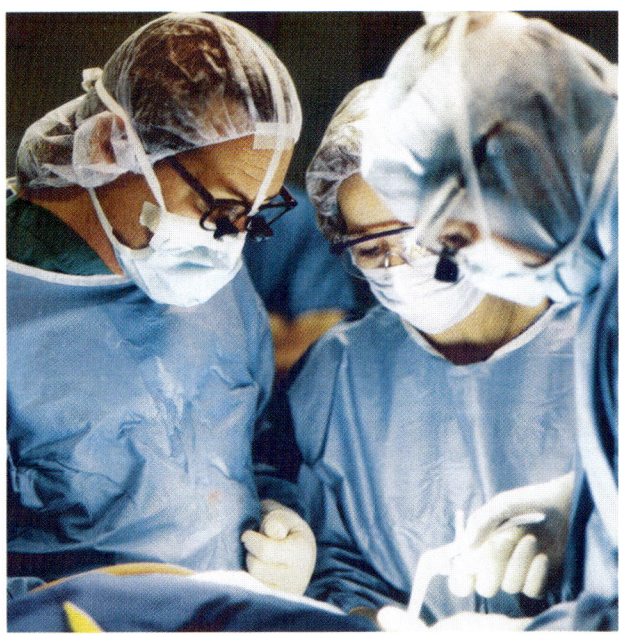

Minimally invasive procedures and leading edge medical imaging technologies complement the hospital's team of specialists and medical expertise.

poor and underserved, the hospital fosters a mission-driven parish-nursing program. Working with community churches, parish nurses (registered nurses) serve as health educators, counselors, and advocates, empowering individuals and groups with tools, facilitating better health and spirituality.

Saint Alphonsus also provides periodic free screenings for prostate and skin cancers, blood pressure, cholesterol levels, and other essential preventative services. These screening services and other critical care programs are supported in large part through the Saint Alphonsus Foundation.

Numerous community events and activities bring much needed health education, awareness, and aid to the community. Among the events that have become synonymous with Saint Alphonsus is the Capitol Classic, a short run/walk for children with all proceeds benefiting children's services. Another race in which Saint Alphonsus is a prime sponsor is the Susan G. Komen Race for the Cure, drawing over 10,000 participants to benefit breast cancer education and awareness. Other events raise funds for the Lions Eye Bank, the Saint Alphonsus Eye Care Center, and related health-care needs. And, as is the tradition in late November, Boise Centre on the Grove is transformed into a winter wonderland through the Saint Alphonsus Festival of Trees. Since 1984, this event has delighted thousands of festival participants and raised over $3.5 million for community and regional health services.

As a tertiary care facility, Saint Alphonsus provides specialized care alongside an array of health and wellness services beyond those illustrated here. From Behavioral Health services to outpatient surgery;

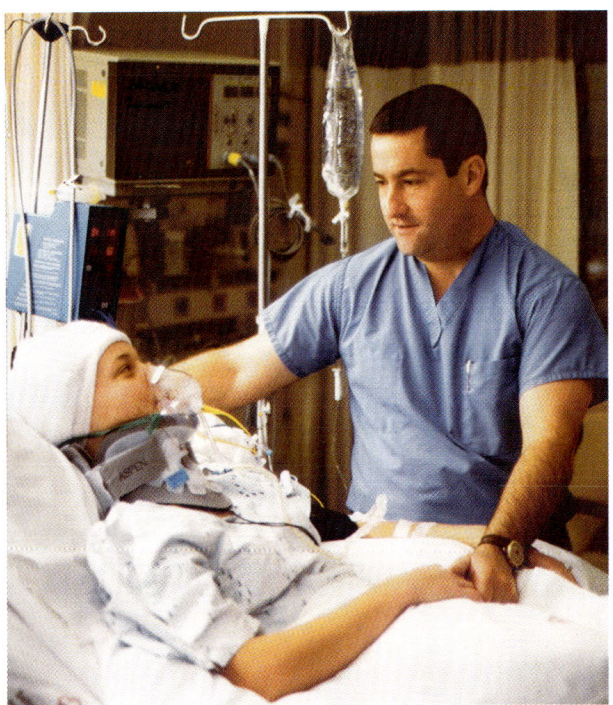

Patients at Saint Alphonsus receive exceptional care to address their physical, emotional, and spiritual needs.

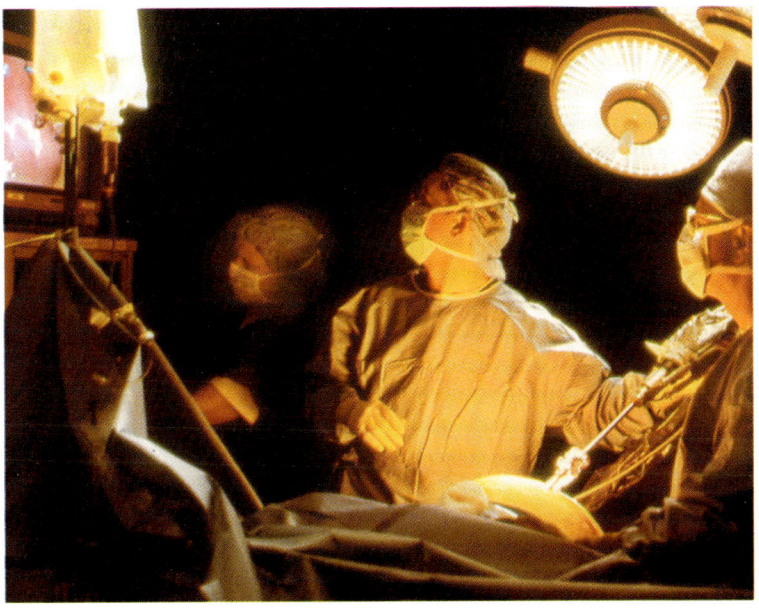

From high-tech to high touch patient care services, Saint Alphonsus continues to focus on the healthcare needs of the community, in the spirit of a faith-based mission.

Home Health to Rehabilitation; Orthopaedics to Pediatrics and beyond, Saint Alphonsus continues to provide advanced healing in these and many other areas. This standard of care—begun over one hundred years ago—will be carried forward as the hospital prepares for the community's future healthcare needs, culminating with Saint Alphonsus' vision—the evolution of a regional healthcare system.

The hospital's plans to meet 21st century needs involve an innovative, integrated healthcare delivery system. By recognizing the diversity of the region's population—from rural communities to downtown corridors, agricultural to high-tech industries, local residents to bordering states—Saint Alphonsus is prepared to deliver healthcare services into the future.

Looking ahead, people will be able to manage their health and wellness from their own home. Empowering self-care, adopting technologies for accessibility to care, and tele-monitoring for schools or work sites are just a few programs the hospital is planning to support to serve the residential needs of tomorrow.

Beyond the home, Saint Alphonsus will look to expand upon the neighborhood health village concept through its network of local physicians and medical clinics. A comprehensive high-tech medical information system that serves patients and physicians, delivered alongside traditional health education, disease management, and related counseling programs is another plan for the future. Through advancements such as tele-medicine, communication technologies will bring faster and more precise delivery of health information and care.

As population centers grow, so do the needs for those requiring little or no hospitalization. Saint Alphonsus will continue to support these needs through urgent care centers—complete with high-tech diagnostic imagery and treatment services alongside outpatient surgical services as determined by the needs of the area—ensuring superior quality of care, independent of time or distance.

Healthcare services in the region will be further enhanced as Saint Alphonsus transforms its current home on Curtis Road into the medical high-tech center of the future and adapts a high-tech, high touch patient care services model. The current 336 bed, 30-year-old facility, built before the information technology age, will be renovated to incorporate an advanced healing environment alongside state-of-the-art devices. The needs of the patient remain the focus, whether through innovative Web tools for drug interactions and disease management protocols or acuity adaptable rooms that provide privacy for patients and their families.

Optimizing the physical, mental and spiritual well being of patients, families, and staff is the hallmark of Saint Alphonsus. This philosophy was established when the hospital first began serving patients over 100 years ago. Saint Alphonsus continues its pioneering spirit and looks ahead to the future to improve the health of the community.

Saint Alphonsus Life Flight is the state's first nationally accredited medical air transportation service, meeting the needs of individuals and emergency medical services in a 100,000-square-mile area around Boise.

Blue Cross of Idaho

Blue Cross of Idaho's mission has remained the same for more than half a century: to provide the best value in health insurance in Idaho. As the oldest and leading health insurer in the state, Blue Cross of Idaho strives each day to promote the delivery of high quality, cost-effective care, while remaining a locally owned financially sound company.

An independent licensee of the Blue Cross and Blue Shield Association, Blue Cross of Idaho is a tax-paying not-for-profit mutual insurance company with more than 300,000 members enrolled in its Traditional, PPO, Managed Care, and Medicare supplement programs, as well as its Medicare + Choice product *TrueBlue®*. At its headquarters in Meridian, Blue Cross of Idaho employs more than 600 employees, with additional staff in its district offices in Coeur d'Alene, Lewiston, Twin Falls, Pocatello, and Idaho Falls.

Blue Cross of Idaho is proud of its Idaho heritage and Idaho focus. The insurer remains locally owned and operated despite industry consolidation that has reduced the number of Blue Plans nationwide from 128 in 1975 to 43 today.

Blue Cross of Idaho is committed to providing its policyholders superior service. In the customer service area alone, employees answer an average of more than 2,000 inquiries a day, as well as

BlueAnn Ewe travels to local elementary schools to teach lessons on healthy eating, exercise, bicycle safety, dental care, and other health and safety topics. Since her debut in 1999, she has visited more than 9,500 students from 51 schools.

Blue Cross of Idaho's Blue Crew participates in a variety of events and activities, including the St. Luke's Women's Fitness Celebration held each September in downtown Boise. Each year, this event attracts 16,000+ participants.

assist walk-in customers who need help. There is never a routine day or routine customer for these employees—every call is an opportunity to provide the best service possible. In fact, Blue Cross of Idaho ranks in the top 25 percent of all Blue Plans nationwide in terms of claims accuracy and turnaround time, enrollment accuracy, and customer service telephone accessibility.

Blue Cross of Idaho is a leader in working cooperatively with community-based provider networks and continues to retain the largest provider networks in Idaho, including 93 percent of all physicians and 98 percent of all hospitals in its Traditional plan, and 79 percent of physicians and 95 percent of hospitals in its PPO plan. This extensive network means that its customers choose their doctors, hospitals, and other health care providers from the state's most comprehensive provider panel.

Because Blue Cross of Idaho recognizes that early detection through screening saves lives, the insurer added wellness benefits, including routine examinations and diagnostic screening tests, to all of its products.

In 1999, Blue Cross of Idaho embarked on a multi-year project to upgrade its core business systems and develop robust Internet and e-commerce capabilities to ensure its independence and competitive position. By the close of 2001, the enrollment, billing, and claims processing functions for two-thirds of its membership had been moved to a new state-of-the-art information system called Facets. Blue Cross of Idaho's Facets implementation places the company on an equal technology footing with some of the largest health care plans in the country.

The information and self-service options available on the bcidaho.com Web site continue to be enhanced with customers, providers, brokers, and the public all benefiting from the growing functionality of the e-health initiatives. Members and business partners are connected through secure Web portals that are customized to meet their specific needs. Customers have access through the Internet to personalized information such as eligibility, benefits, deductible information, and claims status.

Part of Blue Cross of Idaho's commitment to Idahoans also includes its ability to offer resources, time, and teamwork to the communities it serves. For example, through the formation of the Blue Cross of Idaho Foundation for Health, the insurer has dedicated funds to promote wellness and prevention programs available to all Idaho residents. For the past 15 years, Blue Cross of Idaho has participated in the United Way's annual corporate giving campaign. As Blue Cross of Idaho sees it, its employees' contributions make a significant investment toward a healthier community.

Blue Cross of Idaho initiated its BlueAnn Ewe health education program because it recognized the importance of teaching healthy habits to children at an early age. BlueAnn Ewe is Blue Cross of Idaho's health and wellness ambassador. She is a six-foot-tall blue sheep that travels with a health educator to visit first-grade students. Since her debut in April 1999, BlueAnn Ewe has taught lessons on healthy eating, exercise, bicycle safety, dental care, drug danger, and

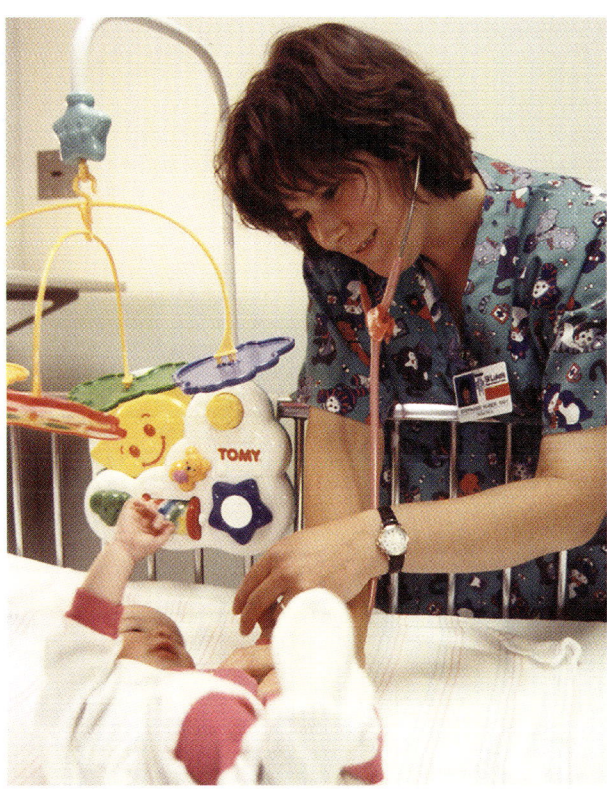

Blue Cross of Idaho's partnerships with community-based provider networks mean that its customers choose their physicians, hospitals, and other health care providers from the state's largest and most comprehensive panel.
Photo courtesy St. Luke's Regional Medical Center

Blue Cross of Idaho members benefit from a variety of special programs and services. Recipe for Life is a free nutrition program for *TrueBlue®* members that includes nutrition sessions with a registered dietician and cooking demonstrations.

other health and safety topics to more than 9,500 students from 51 schools. Blue Cross of Idaho works with elementary educators who continue to find the presentation memorable and effective while also meeting their health curriculum standards.

In 1999, Blue Cross of Idaho formalized its Blue Crew employee volunteer program. The Blue Crew offers coordinated opportunities for positive teamwork experiences and community service projects. The Blue Crew mobilizes a team of volunteers for a variety of events including fitness runs and walks to raise funds and awareness for causes such as juvenile diabetes and breast cancer. Following the tragic events of September 11, the Blue Crew not only donated blood, but also initiated a fundraising effort to support the American Red Cross National Disaster Relief Fund.

As Blue Cross of Idaho moves through the new millennium, staying connected to its customers and to the communities within Idaho will remain one of the insurer's highest priorities. By adapting quickly to the health care marketplace demands and offering new solutions and choices for its customers—through product development, benefit plan options, improved technology, and customer service—Blue Cross of Idaho will continue to be the clear choice for high-quality, customer-focused, innovative, and affordable health care coverage.

St. Luke's Regional Medical Center

100 Years of Caring

St. Luke's has been caring for the Boise community since 1902 when the Rt. Rev. James B. Funsten, an Episcopal bishop and missionary, recognized the city's need for "sufficient proper facilities for the care of the sick."

Bishop Funsten founded St. Luke's as a six-bed frontier hospital, located at the same downtown site where St. Luke's Regional Medical Center can be found today. From this humble beginning, St. Luke's has grown to become Idaho's largest healthcare provider, with three full-service hospitals. St. Luke's has the state's first and most experienced newborn intensive care unit and cancer and heart treatment centers, as well as more than 25 outpatient clinics and diagnostic centers. Also specializing in women and children's services, St. Luke's provides care to hundreds of thousands of patients each year from across a multi-state region.

St. Luke's founder, the Rt. Rev. James B. Funsten, with graduating nurses, circa 1912.

The days of the horse-drawn ambulance and doctors making house calls by buggy are over, but St. Luke's future is firmly rooted in the past—in a tradition of excellence spanning more than 100 years.

Since the time that St. Luke's cared for its first patient and saw families through smallpox and diphtheria, polio, war, and the Great Depression, a lot has changed, especially in the realm of technology. The people of Boise and the surrounding area have long relied on St. Luke's to provide the latest, most innovative and effective medical treatment. In recent years, St. Luke's has introduced state-of-the-art technology to Idaho that Bishop Funsten, with all his foresightedness, could not have imagined. To enhance cancer diagnosis, St. Luke's was the first to bring positron emission tomography (PET) scanning and R2 ImageChecker technology to Boise. The first open heart surgery in Idaho was performed here in 1968 and the state's only children's hospital is located within St. Luke's Regional Medical Center. But even in today's technological world, St. Luke's focus is always on the patient—a never-ending tribute to the spirit of compassion inherent in its origins.

This compassion extends to all areas of St. Luke's, springing from a selfless and philanthropic community whose dedication to St. Luke's mission, "to improve the health of people in our region," has helped create one of the finest hospitals in the country. It is because of the support of generous benefactors and thousands of volunteers, past and present, that St. Luke's is able to meet the medical care needs of a diverse populace—from critically ill babies to teens with cancer to seniors with cardiovascular disease.

A Century of Nursing Excellence

Over the years, St. Luke's has earned many national awards, from being honored as one of the nation's Top 100 hospitals to

After one hundred years, St. Luke's is still located on its original site at the corner of 1st and Bannock Streets.

being named by Idaho consumers as the hospital with best overall quality, best doctors and nurses, and best image and reputation. Since the time that St. Luke's School of Nursing was founded (also by Bishop Funsten) shortly after the hospital opened its doors, St. Luke's nurses have been known for their kindness, expertise, and exceptional bedside care. Today, St. Luke's is Idaho's only Magnet Hospital, a prestigious national designation that recognizes nursing excellence and quality patient care.

Opening Doors…and Hospitals

No person is ever denied care at St. Luke's, regardless of ability to pay—an open door policy that embraces Bishop Funsten's original vision. As a non-profit organization, St. Luke's returns every net dollar earned back to the community through building improvements, the latest technology, and medical equipment upgrades. This commitment has meant an expansion of the hospital system beyond the city of Boise to the growing communities of Meridian and the Wood River Valley.

Inside and Out, St. Luke's Cares

Along with the exceptional care it provides, St. Luke's is recognized by many Boiseans as one of the city's aesthetic jewels. The hospital's downtown location presents challenges for growth, but these have been met with particular attention to beauty. The hospital's interior was designed with the patient in mind—from soothing colors on floors and walls to light and spacious waiting areas. And the highest of architectural standards, combined with preservation of historic buildings, creates a charming blend of the old and the new. Hundreds of flowerbeds, century-old ivy, and countless trees provide color through all the seasons, while the timeless red brick

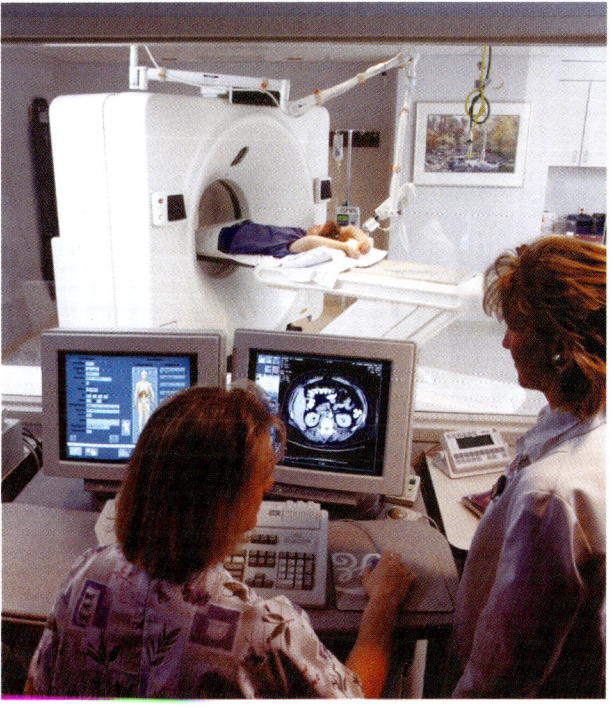

St. Luke's combines expert staff with continual advancements in medical science.

that is St. Luke's hallmark graces buildings in a ten-block area from Avenue B to Fourth Street.

A Lasting Commitment to the Community

Whether creating a homelike, yet technologically advanced environment for premature infants, installing the latest radiation therapy equipment, or enhancing hospital stays with pet therapy, St. Luke's never loses sight of what matters most—the person with medical needs. That's why St. Luke's does its best to educate men, women, and children regarding disease prevention and the importance of healthy lifestyle habits. From its quarterly magazine to its award-winning Web site to sponsorship of the St. Luke's Celebration—one of the largest women-only health and fitness events in the country—St. Luke's is committed to healing and, above all, good health for the entire community.

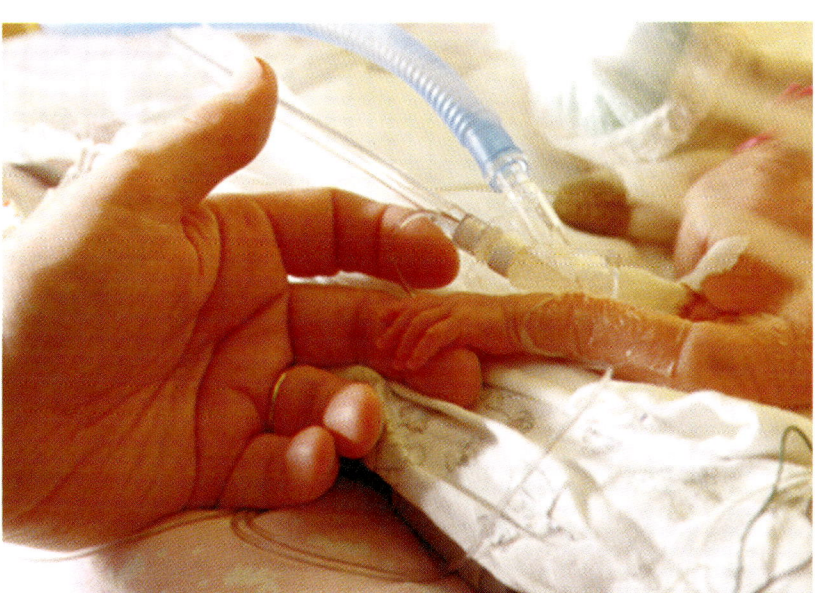

Technology and tender loving care are specialties at St. Luke's Children's Hospital.

Boise Heart Clinic

The Boise Heart Clinic, founded by James W. Smith, M.D., was Idaho's first cardiology group and has remained on the cutting edge of cardiac care for over 25 years. The clinic's group of board certified physicians offers a full range of cardiovascular services to patients throughout Idaho and eastern Oregon.

Each of the clinic's physicians brings an area of cardiac expertise to the practice. Dr. James W. Smith, an Idaho native, studied cardiology at the University of California, Los Angeles and currently serves on the State Board of Medicine.

Dr. Charles M. Rasmussen joined the clinic after earning a fellowship in cardiovascular diseases and specialized training in echocardiographic and noninvasive procedures at the University of California, San Diego.

Dr. Robert S. Lee completed a cardiology fellowship at the University of Southern California and an advanced fellowship with the Cardiology Center in New Orleans focusing on interventional procedures.

Dr. Donald K. Stott, the first board-certified cardiologist in Idaho, has a wealth of experience in diagnostic and interventional procedures. He joined his practice with the Boise Heart Clinic in 1995.

Dr. David F. Oakes received fellowship training in electrophysiology at Tufts University in Boston. He specializes in treating cardiac rhythm problems and in implanting pacemakers and defibrillators.

The diverse professional backgrounds of this group enable Boise Heart Clinic to offer a wide range of specialized care. The clinic is the only practice in Idaho that provides External CounterPulsation (ECP) therapy, a non-invasive treatment for chronic angina pectoris, and is involved in researching ECP as a treatment for congestive heart failure. In addition to this, Boise Heart Clinic was one of the first clinics in the country to utilize radiation therapy to enhance the benefits of coronary stents.

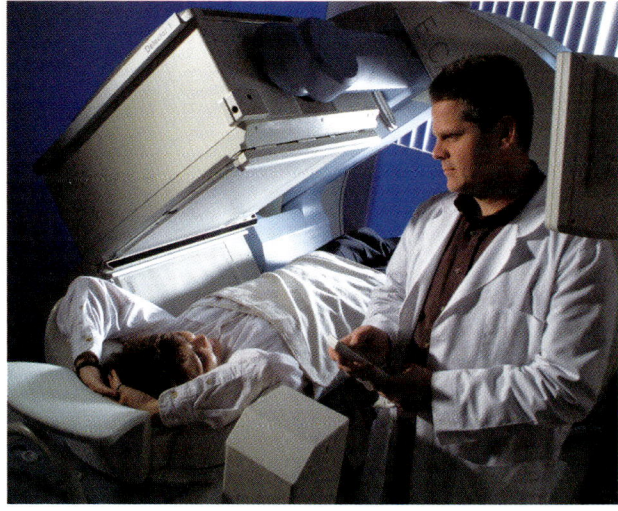

At Boise Heart Clinic, excellence in health care means providing the latest in technological advances while treating each patient with personal service and compassion.

The clinic's superb nursing staff, supervised by Francis Addy, R.N., and dedicated administrative staff, led by Jacqueline Bruns, reflect the physicians' determination to provide personalized, professional care in a welcoming atmosphere. The practice has grown to meet the needs of an expanding patient base and operates clinics in Boise, Meridian, and Emmett. The clinic's physicians not only work with St. Luke's Regional Medical Center and Saint Alphonsus Medical Center, but with outlying area hospitals as well.

The physicians at the Boise Heart Clinic are strongly dedicated to serving Idaho's cardiac needs and their highly individualized patient care has earned them a respected position in the medical community.

Providing Boise with superior personal cardiac care is the primary goal of the Boise Heart Clinic. Pictured are (seated left to right) Dr. Donald K. Stott and Dr. James W. Smith; (standing left to right) Dr. Robert S. Lee, Dr. Charles M. Rasmussen, and Dr. David F. Oakes.

Regence BlueShield of Idaho

With over 650 employees serving more than 275,000 members, Regence BlueShield of Idaho stands tall as the leading health insurer in the state.

Its roots were established in 1946 by 27 physicians of the North Idaho Medical Society, who each provided contributions of $100, thus incorporating the North Idaho District Medical Service Bureau on February 20, 1946 as a way to establish a method of prepaid medical insurance. By 1950, the company was operating in nine of the 10 North Idaho counties. Three years later, it had 25,000 insureds and 400 companies utilizing its varied policies. By the 1960s, the company had joined the national and regional Blue Shield association of physician-sponsored prepaid medical service plans.

While Medical Service Bureau, as it was then known, was founded in Lewiston and began business primarily in the northern part of the state, the company decided to expand statewide in the 1970s. When the company was awarded the contract for the State of Idaho in 1976, offices were opened in Boise, as well as in all other areas of the state, and the company added Blue Shield of Idaho to its name.

Since then, Regence BlueShield of Idaho, as it is now known, has served as the health insurance provider for the State of Idaho. As the major population center in the state, it has proven beneficial that Regence BlueShield of Idaho became a part of Boise and the entire Treasure Valley. By offering a variety of health-insurance plans to individuals and groups, Regence BlueShield of Idaho has been able to give consumers the ability to take control of their health-care choices.

The increasing demand for lower-cost health care has resulted in Regence BlueShield of Idaho creating new and innovative insurance products that emphasize wellness and preventive care and are designed to help physicians, employers and individuals better manage health-care dollars. Such products as Defined Contribution, an online enrollment program, and the company's BlueCard, which assures members the best in health care while traveling across the country and abroad, have proven to be instrumental in providing members with the highest quality health care while still managing to control costs.

Regence BlueShield of Idaho takes great pride in its role toward the continued growth of the community. Executive staff members participate in the political process and help protect the interest of members by communicating the company's positions on health care to legislators who have the ultimate decision on the outcome of state and federal health-care legislation. Elected officials are kept informed about how their decisions dramatically impact the everyday work lives of Regence BlueShield of Idaho members. Through its Corporate Giving Committee and employee volunteerism, the company strives to play a role in the communities in which it serves.

A great deal has changed since the early days of Regence BlueShield of Idaho. In the past, Indemnity and fee-for-service programs along with Medicare supplements provided basic benefits and standard options, as did hospitalization room and board. Today, there is more variety and broader coverage in benefits and services such as Preferred Provider Organization products, point of service products, and Medicare managed care products, which have all been designed to provide the best care for each policyholder. Programs such as the Employee/Individual Assistance programs, Integrated Behavioral Health programs, and Maternity Management offer peace of mind to those members requiring special care in those areas. A 24-hour nurse line and audio health library are also offered to members, as is a host of proactive care management services.

Change is inevitable in the health-insurance industry. Regence BlueShield of Idaho embraces change and continues to move forward as the industry does. The company will continue to provide the best possible health coverage that has made it the leading health insurer in the state since 1946.

Regence BlueShield of Idaho plans to continue growing along with Boise by offering health-insurance benefits, services, and support to its members. With a strong leadership role in the community, as well as the company, Regence BlueShield of Idaho will continue to operate as the leading health insurer in the state and be prepared to shape and mold the health insurance industry in order for it to reach its highest potential in the 21st century.

Regence BlueShield of Idaho takes pride in being the leading health insurer in the state of Idaho.

11

The Marketplace, Hospitality & Tourism

WestCoast ParkCenter Suites, 154

AmeriSuites, 156

The Bon Marché, 158

Meridian Ford, 160

Karen Louise Fashion Boutique, 161

Photo © Patrick Teglia

WestCoast ParkCenter Suites

WestCoast ParkCenter Suites utilizes a unique lodging concept that combines the convenience of a prime ParkCenter location with the comfort of home-like amenities. Just five minutes from downtown, ten minutes from the airport, and adjacent to the scenic Boise River Greenbelt, the relaxed park location is perfect for business or pleasure.

Since its inception in 1992, WestCoast ParkCenter Suites has committed itself to a high level of customer service by providing an outstanding value, along with meticulously clean and well-appointed accommodations. The friendly, obliging staff is always willing to assist guests with special requests and services. Whether in search of a nearby restaurant or a challenging golf course, assistance is just a phone call away.

For WestCoast ParkCenter Suites, part of being your home away from home is offering a room that fits your needs. Each of the 238 spacious suites offers the convenience of kitchen facilities, including a microwave, refrigerator, toaster, coffee maker with complimentary coffee, china, and flatware. In addition to a generous living space with parson's table and sofa sleeper, each suite offers an in-room food and beverage bar, full-size iron and ironing board, hair dryer, two telephones, and a 25" television with in-room movies. For the corporate or leisure traveler who needs to stay connected, WestCoast ParkCenter Suites offers free local phone calls, voicemail service, and wireless high-speed Internet access.

It has been said that breakfast is the most important meal of the day, and at WestCoast ParkCenter Suites, they take it seriously. Included with each stay is a complimentary deluxe continental breakfast, featuring freshly-baked pastries, bagels, croissants, muffins,

Executive Quarters guests enjoy a private lounge with complimentary beverages and hors d'oeuvres served each evening.

waffles, yogurt, fresh fruit, cold cereal, hot cereal, coffee, tea, and an assortment of juices. While enjoying breakfast, guests may keep up to date on current events by perusing a complimentary newspaper.

WestCoast ParkCenter Suites wants to provide a stay that is both relaxing and memorable. Guests can enjoy a workout in the fitness center, take a dip in the heated outdoor pool, or relax in the year-round outdoor Jacuzzi. Guests who value nature can take a leisurely stroll on the Boise Greenbelt, which offers wonderful views of the Boise River and indigenous wildlife. Bike rental is also available through area businesses for a longer excursion. For the kid in all of us, a video arcade provides hours of challenging entertainment. The aroma of freshly baked cookies greets guests each evening as they enter the hotel lobby, where they can also enjoy snacks and drinks in the lobby bar between 5:30 and 10:00 p.m.

WestCoast ParkCenter Suites, located in the scenic ParkCenter Business District.

WestCoast ParkCenter Suites offers conveniently located laundry facilities in addition to same-day dry-cleaning services. Courtesy airport shuttle and express checkout take the hassle out of traveling.

For the guest who appreciates being pampered by the little extras, WestCoast ParkCenter Suites offers concierge-level suites. These suites feature complimentary hors d'oeuvres, beer and wine served nightly in the exclusive Executive Quarters Lounge, as well as a complimentary upgraded continental breakfast buffet served each morning. Guests are welcome to enjoy 24-hour access to complimentary snacks, sodas, juices, and bottled water.

Taking care of business is a pleasure when it's done at WestCoast ParkCenter Suites. WestCoast ParkCenter Suites is perfectly equipped to host a variety of events, and our highly trained banquet staff ensures your meeting will run seamlessly. WestCoast ParkCenter Suites boasts five executive conference rooms, totaling nearly 2000 square feet, connecting to an outdoor courtyard that provides ample natural sunlight. For smaller groups, the Executive Boardroom provides deluxe accommodations.

You are invited to experience WestCoast hospitality at any one of over 90 WestCoast or Red Lion Hotels throughout the western United States. Frequent guests are invited to join WestAwards™, our guest reward program. This program offers guests who stay frequently at WestCoast and Red Lion Hotels a chance to earn points toward complimentary hotel nights, air travel, entertainment tickets, merchandise, and more. Guests can enjoy the flexibility of earning points for every eligible dollar charged to their room and easily redeem their points through WestAwards Guest Services.

A commitment to service and value, along with its convenient location for business and recreation, makes WestCoast ParkCenter Suites synonymous with comfort and value. When traveling to Boise, WestCoast ParkCenter Suites is the hotel of choice. ■

A distinctive style and comfort greet guests staying at WestCoast ParkCenter Suites.

The heated seasonal lap pool and year-round Jacuzzi provide relaxation and fun.

AmeriSuites

When a customer first walks into the Boise AmeriSuites, they instantly know that they have chosen the best all-suite hotel in the area. From the rich burgundy colors, which dominate the décor, to the grandiose chandelier that illuminates the entire lobby, the people at AmeriSuites take their customers' desires for a comfortable and relaxing atmosphere very seriously.

First opened in January of 1999, the people at AmeriSuites understand that their customers want the closest experience possible to being at home while they happen to be away from home. That is why all of the 128 occupancies available at AmeriSuites have been constructed as suites. Each suite comes equipped with all the amenities of home including an iron and ironing board, hair dryer, refrigerator, microwave and wet bar, coffee maker with complimentary coffee, voice mail service, and even laundry and valet services available to each of AmeriSuites' customers. Free local transportation is also offered as well as transportation to and from the airport. There is also a fitness center on the grounds where visitors can get a complete cardiovascular workout as well as a heated indoor pool for those looking for a relaxing climate-controlled swim. Each suite also comes equipped with a large 26" cable television and video cassette player for visitors that need a little rest and relaxation after a long day or they can sit back in one of the suite's comfortable chairs and peruse over a complimentary copy of *USA Today*. These luxuries combined with a complimentary bountiful breakfast buffet complete with 27 delicious items give each of its customers the comforts of home and more.

Bountiful Breakfast Buffet™.

AmeriSuites recognizes that many of its customers are staying with them as part of a business trip and may need even more amenities readily available at their fingertips. Therefore, 41 of the 128 suites are referred to as TCB Suites, or "Taking Care of Business" Suites. Several key points differentiate the TCB Suite from the standard suites available, including two-line speakerphones with data ports so that customers can work on-line and conduct business simultaneously. An oversized executive desk in the room combined with an upholstered executive chair gives visitors plenty of space to spread out their projects and work comfortably. A Smart Lamp with additional receptacles for office electronics is available in the TCB Suites so that electrical items can be plugged in with ease. Each desk comes readily supplied with office supplies, snacks to keep the customer going on those late-night projects and a side desk return on wheels that can be adjusted to fit your needs. And when you add an oversized leisure chair and ottoman for kicking back and relaxing, there's little wonder that a TCB Suite beats a day at the office on any day. In addition, for those business people who need an even larger area than the suites

Boise's Premium Choice "All-Suite" Hotel.

Lobby/guest services.

to convene in, the hotel has a 950-square-foot meeting room that holds up to 80 people comfortably.

With all these extras that a customer would not normally expect from a hotel stay, it's refreshing to know that the staff at AmeriSuites still relies on the basics to keep their customers happy. Treating each customer fairly and kindly has been the hotel's number one concern since its inception. The staff realizes that the customers are not staying at the hotel simply for its clean rooms and wealth of amenities alone but for the friendly and reliable service that every AmeriSuites across the country believes in. Oftentimes, it doesn't matter to the customer what toll a hotel room may take on the wallet; as long as guests are comfortable and made to feel welcome, they feel that they have received their money's worth. When the customer has been treated with the utmost respect, the chances of them coming back for a return visit is almost inevitable.

Having a central location minutes off the freeway has helped make AmeriSuites the success that it has become in such a short time. Within walking distance to Boise Town Square, the hotel is perfect for families as well as business travelers. Several activities geared toward families are located on the AmeriSuites grounds or nearby, including bicycling/jogging trails, children's activities, nature preserves/trails, a theater, billiards and snooker, several fine dining choices, and museums and galleries.

The AmeriSuites in Boise is currently the only one of its kind in the Northwest area. The decision to come to Boise was made after it was determined that Boise's growth pattern showed that there was more demand for hotels in the area. With more people coming to the city every day, the corporation feels that its decision to be represented in Boise was a wise one.

Striving for a "friendly" reputation amongst the local hotel industry, AmeriSuites is always willing to help out the community at large. Whether it's being productive members of the Boise Chamber of Commerce or collecting donations for the Red Cross in times of need, AmeriSuites recognizes the importance of the continued success of the community and is always willing to do its share to help maintain a healthy relationship with the people of Boise.

With a commitment to friendly service and the comfort of its customers, it's little wonder that AmeriSuites serves as the cornerstone of Boise's hospitality.

Comfortable, spacious suites.

The Bon Marché

"Good deal"

These two words form a loose translation for the French term Bon Marché, a name that has become synonymous with quality in the Boise area for the last 40 years.

The Seattle-based department store chain is the namesake of a Paris store, which was founded by Aristide Boucicaut, a French merchant who has been credited with inventing the very first department store. Today, The Bon Marché stands tall as a retailing innovator in the Pacific Northwest region, with a superb track record of serving major metropolitan and mid-sized communities in Washington, Oregon, Idaho, Montana, and Wyoming. While the majority of The Bon Marché's 44 stores are in Washington, Boise has served as the home for two of the chain's more successful stores since 1962.

The downtown Boise Bon Marché opened its doors in 1896, originally operating as a Golden Rule store. The store's name was later changed to C.C. Anderson after its founder and moved to Main Street. Mr. Anderson was a native of Missouri who was trained alongside James Cash Penney, who also shortened his name to his initials and opened up his own retail store that he named after himself—J.C. Penney. Anderson's first foray into the world of retail was in Colorado, but when the state's high altitudes began to affect his health he decided to relocate and move to Boise, bringing his smart sense of business with him and forever changing the retail landscape in the city.

For 26 years, The Bon Marché has been instrumental in providing leadership among the retailers in the downtown area. In 1988, it broadened its horizons by becoming one of the main anchor stores at the new Boise Towne Square Mall, yet choosing to keep its historic downtown store open for business, thus creating a powerful recognition factor in Boise's two strongest retail markets. As several of the downtown merchants began closing their doors and relocating to the Towne Square area, The Bon Marché remained one of the few stores that stayed downtown, helping to keep the downtown area alive at a time when its future looked bleak. During the second expansion of the Towne Square Mall location which left the sprawling store with 180,000 square feet of retail space, the Mayor publicly thanked The Bon Marché for having the faith to keep its downtown location open thus playing a pivotal role in the revitalization of downtown Boise and proving to be a trusted partner with the city.

Serving as an integral partner to the city and community has always been an important facet of The Bon Marché and its employees. Each year, The Bon Marché donates time, money, and services to several different charities and organizations throughout the Boise area. Recognizing the importance of adults being properly educated in order to maintain employment, The Bon Marché has donated several thousand dollars to Learning Lab.

The retail giant has also made substantial contributions to other organizations. Committed to involving employees in their communities, the Downtown Boise store has volunteered for the Boise Art Museum, worked with St. Luke's, participated in "Rake Up Boise," "Paint The Town," and many of its employees spend

Downtown Boise Bon Marché Furniture Associate Carol Herring (left) is one of the many BONpeople who make The Bon Marché the best place to work and the best place to shop in Boise.

Nestled in the heart of Boise, The Bon Marché has served the community for over 40 years, not only helping to cultivate the downtown shopping experience, but also giving back through its Partners in Time outreach program.

one hour each week tutoring elementary school children. And for the past decade, The Bon Marché has served as a major sponsor of the annual Boise River Festival, playing a vital role in the Festival to ensure its continued success as one of the premier events in the city each year.

The hard work and dedication that each of its 79 employees give back into the community has paid off in various ways. The United Way has cited The Bon as being the best retail store in Boise when it comes to its role towards the betterment of the community. Being honored in such a tremendous way is not only a testament to the superior quality of the employees, but also it serves as a foundation on which to continue building strong customer loyalties. As the decades of service that The Bon Marché has provided continue to grow, the customer's expectations for quality, honesty, and service have never waned. There has always been a certain level of trust in that The Bon Marché will provide the best customer service and the best shopping experience. It's what is simply referred to as "BONlife."

BONlife drives The Bon Marché and makes the company an employer of choice. It is the name given to the daily operations of the company and its employees. BONlife puts a strong emphasis on work/life balance for its employees, giving BONpeople the opportunity to lead a balanced life and enjoy coming to work each day. Through BONvalues, an established set of six core values including respect, balance, and high standards, BONlife strengthened employee retention and is truly a "ground up" process that encourages employees to pursue both a successful career and happy family life.

BONlife is The Bon Marché's brand—to its external customers as well as its employees. BON=good is another handle that The Bon turned into an effective marketing technique. Now, instead of "good deal", the Bon Marché offers "BONdeals," and rather than "good gifts," the store offers its customers "BONgifts." The Bon adopted the BONlife tagline "it's everything good for life...for you" as a way to communicate to its customers what BONlife is all about: "an attitude and style of communicating...that conveyed **BON**people living, thinking and feeling **BON**life."

BONlife...making The Bon Marché the best place to work and the best place to shop...every day.

Meridian Ford

As the saying goes, Meridian Ford has been in the business of making friends since 1960. That was the year Hoot Gibson and Roger Welker first opened the Ford dealership in the small town of Meridian with 17 employees on the payroll. In 1979, Larry Chetwood bought the business and today is the sole proprietor of the dealership that has grown beyond anyone's visions. Resting on nine acres with a 35,000-square-foot facility, Meridian Ford now employs 70 people and has earned more awards from the Ford Motor Company than any other Ford dealer in Idaho. The growth and success of Meridian Ford mirrors the spectacular growth that the City of Meridian has experienced over the last decade.

Many Treasure Valley residents know the company by its 80-foot-high electronic sign that serves as its trademark, but it is the company's commitment to service that has secured the loyalty of its customers. The dealership offers such luxuries as giving its customers a free service loaner car every time that their car is admitted into the shop overnight for the life of the car, which has helped boost customer retention and repeat business.

Meridian Ford has over 300 vehicles in its inventory and has successfully launched its quality-checked certified pre-owned

Meridian Ford's freeway location can be easily identified by their signature logo sign.

vehicle program. These vehicles are reconditioned to factory specs, come with a 6-year, 75,000-mile warranty, and have proven themselves to be a major portion of Meridian's success.

The awards that Meridian Ford has received include the prestigious President's Award and the most recent Blue Oval Certification. These reflect the mindset of how the business feels about its customers and how that feeling permeates the entire organization.

This caring nature overflows into the dealership's relationship with the community as a whole. Larry Chetwood is the past president of the Meridian Education Foundation, which funds a large number of teacher's projects. Meridian Ford also supports the Salvation Army, the Hope House, the Idaho Youth Ranch, the United Way of Treasure Valley, the Meridian Boys and Girls Club, and several other organizations.

Meridian Ford plans to continue growing and has land-banked two acres of its property for future expansion. Because in the company's quest to remain the most successful Ford dealership in the state, the Chetwoods know that nothing can be done half-heartedly in this business. Those dealerships that don't maintain a commitment to impeccable customer relations and outstanding service will end up hurting the auto industry. And it's that line of thinking that has helped write the success story of Meridian Ford.

Meridian Ford's showroom.

Karen Louise Fashion Boutique

At Karen Louise, the general opinion is that "if they look fabulous, they'll be back." Owner Karen Louise Falk believes it's important to feel good in the clothes one wears. With such a high level of fashion and quality involved, this is one goal that is met on a regular basis at Karen Louise Fashion Boutique in Boise's historic downtown district.

Located in the heart of Old Boise, Karen Louise Fashion Boutique brings a "touch of class" to the ladies of Idaho's capital city, providing elegant fashions with individual attention that is often missing from larger stores. Karen Falk's specialty boutique has uptown class, exploring the fine art of fashion in a pristine and relaxed atmosphere.

Falk spent several years in education as an elementary library media coordinator in the Boise area. Once her sons were grown, she opted to pursue a new career. Having always loved Boise's downtown for its rich history and tasteful beauty, Karen began working in various boutiques learning the trade. In 1994, she had an opportunity to buy the business, giving the boutique a chic look and naming it after herself. Since then, Karen has enjoyed a steady demand for the boutique's unique offerings from both locals and out of state women who travel long distances to purchase the very latest in fashion. Karen also schedules several buying trips throughout the year with best friend and husband, Lloyd. They travel around the globe to find the highest quality items and newest fashion trends to bring home to Boise.

Karen Louise takes great pride in being able to help ladies feel good about themselves by dressing them in the highest fashion. Karen provides customers with not only proper clothing, but also matching accessories of hats, shoes, and handbags. By providing a personal, special touch, Karen is able to give each customer complete satisfaction with their choices.

Karen Falk has played an active role in Idaho's capital city for several decades. As a member of the Board of the Downtown Boise

We master the art of being unique. *Photo by Erik Stern*

Association, Karen has conducted several small business seminars for business owners in conjunction with the Boise Chamber of Commerce, always maintaining a vested interest in keeping a clean, safe, and vibrant city for the entire population. In addition, she has remained a Sustainer of the Junior League of Boise and has won several awards throughout the years, including winning the Idaho State Girl of the Year from Epsilon Sigma Alpha (Beta Nu Chapter), Portrait of a Distinguished Citizen from *The Idaho Statesman*, and commissioned a Kentucky Colonel by the Commonwealth of Kentucky.

Karen's keen sense of fashion has also proved instrumental in her role as a longtime judge of scholarship pageants on both local and state levels, as well as individual consultation with contestants through the Miss America Organization. Karen Louise Fashion Boutique includes a "Miss America" room, which displays many of the contestants Karen has been privileged to judge.

Karen enjoys helping her clients to coordinate all of their fashion needs for any event, from casual to black tie. *Photo by Erik Stern*

Enterprise Index

AmeriSuites
925 North Milwaukee
Boise, Idaho 83704
Phone: 208-375-1200
Fax: 208-375-2900
E-mail: losmbo@primehospitality.com
www.amerisuites.com
Pages 156-157

Atwood-Hinzman-Jones
4800 Fairview Avenue
Boise, Idaho 83706
Phone: 208-323-0199
Fax: 208-375-5251
E-mail: ahj@ahjengineers.com
www.ahjengineers.com
Page 120

Blue Cross of Idaho
3000 East Pine Avenue
Meridian, Idaho 83642
Phone: 208-345-4550
E-mail: info@bcidaho.com
www.bcidaho.com
Pages 146-147

Boise Heart Clinic
287 West Jefferson Street
Boise, Idaho 83702
Phone: 208-343-7940
Fax: 208-385-7708
Page 150

The Boise Metro Chamber of Commerce
250 South 5th Street, Suite 800
Post Office Box 2368
Boise, Idaho 83701
Phone: 208-472-5200
Fax: 208-472-5201
E-mail: info@boisechamber.org
www.boisechamber.org
Pages 110-111

The Bon Marché
918 Idaho Street
Boise, Idaho 83702
Phone: 208-388-6008
Fax: 208-388-6007
www.thebon.com
Pages 158-159

Building Materials Holding Corporation
720 Park Boulevard
Suite 200
Boise, Idaho 83712
Phone: 208-331-4300
Fax: 208-331-4382
E-mail: thomas@bmhc.com
www.bmhc.com
Page 101

CH2M HILL
700 Clearwater Lane
Boise, Idaho 83712
Phone: 208-345-5310
Fax: 208-345-5315
E-mail: mbowen@ch2m.com
www.ch2m.com
Page 121

CM Company, Inc.
431 West McGregor Drive
Boise, Idaho 83705
Phone: 208-384-0800
Fax: 208-345-5323
E-mail: cm@cmcompany.com
www.cmcompany.com
Page 139

DIRECTV Boise Customer Contact Center
Post Office Box 70014
Boise, Idaho 83707-0114
Phone: 208-363-6000
           800-347-3288
Fax: 208-363-6349
www.directv.com
Page 100

F&C Corporation and Rocky Mountain Management & Development, LLC
2700 Airport Way
Boise, Idaho 83705
Phone: 208-345-7030
Fax: 208-345-7210
E-mail: mfery@innamerica.com
Page 138

Great West Casualty Company
8757 West Emerald Street
Boise, Idaho 83704
Phone: 208-377-1234
Fax: 208-377-7123
E-mail: v.card@gwccnet.com
www.gwccnet.com
Page 114

habitec
255 North Market Street, #220
San Jose, California 95110
Phone: 408-977-0606
Fax: 408-298-4245
www.habitec.com
Page 124

Hawley Troxell Ennis & Hawley LLP
877 Main Street
Suite 1000
Boise, Idaho 83702
Phone: 208-344-6000
Fax: 208-342-3829
E-mail: saf@hteh.com
www.hteh.com
Page 123

Hewlett-Packard
11311 Chinder Boulevard
Boise, Idaho 83714
Phone: 208-396-6000
www.hp.com
Pages 98-99

Holland & Hart LLP
101 South Capitol Boulevard
Suite 1400
Boise, Idaho 83702
Phone: 208-342-5000
Fax: 208-343-8869
www.hollandhartidaho.com
Pages 118-119

John L. Scott Real Estate
6223 North Discovery Way
Suite 100
Boise, Idaho 83713
Phone: 208-323-4000
Fax: 208-323-0128
www.johnlscott.com
Pages 134-135

Karen Louise Fashion Boutique
625 Main
Boise, Idaho 83702
Phone: 208-385-7915
Fax: 208-385-7903
E-mail: karenlouise@qwest.net
Page 161

KeyBank
702 West Idaho
Boise, Idaho 83702
Phone: 208-364-8751
Fax: 208-364-8756
E-mail: nancy_choules@keybank.com
www.key.com
Page 113

Leatham-Krohn-Van Ocker, Architects
1735 Federal Way
Boise, Idaho 83705
Phone: 208-336-3443
Fax: 208-336-3680
E-mail: lkv@lkvarchitects.com
www.lkvarchitects.com
Page 122

Meridian Ford
250 East Overland Road
Meridian, Idaho 83642
Phone: 208-888-4403
Fax: 208-888-4215
E-mail: lchetwood@meridianford.com
www.meridianford.com
Page 160

Petra
9056 West Blackeagle Drive
Boise, Idaho 83709
Phone: 208-323-4500
Fax: 208-323-4507
E-mail: jfrank@petracontractors.com
www.petracontractors.com
Pages 136-137

Regence BlueShield of Idaho
1602 21st Avenue
Lewiston, Idaho 83501
Phone: 208-746-2671
Fax: 208-798-2087
www.id.regence.com
Page 151

Saint Alphonsus Regional Medical Center
1055 North Curtis Road
Boise, Idaho 83706 1370
Phone: 208-367-2121
www.saintalphonsus.org
Pages 142-145

St. Luke's Regional Medical Center
190 East Bannock
Boise, Idaho 83712
Phone: 208-381-2222
www.stlukesonline.org
Pages 148-149

Steed Construction
1250 East Iron Eagle Drive, #200
Eagle, Idaho 83616
Phone: 208-378-7300
Fax: 208-378-7332
E-mail: sandy.moore@steedconst.com
www.steedconst.com
Pages 128-131

Thornton Oliver Keller
250 South Fifth Street
Second Floor
Boise, Idaho 83702
Phone: 208-378-4600
Fax: 208-947-0869
E-mail: jabarber@tokre.com
www.tokre.com
Pages 132-133

Time Warner Telecom
199 North Capitol Boulevard
Suite 503
Boise, Idaho 83702
Phone: 208-472-4400
Fax: 208-472-4410
E-mail: boiseoffice@twtelecom.com
www.twtelecom.com
Page 102

United Heritage
707 East United Heritage Court
Meridian, Idaho 83642-3527
Phone: 208-493-6100
E-mail: heritage@unitedheritage.com
www.unitedheritage.com
Pages 106-109

Wells Fargo
119 North 9th Street
#U1801-026
Boise, Idaho 83702
Phone: 208-393-2079
Fax: 208-393-2187
E-mail: ckeller@wellsfargo.com
www.wellsfargo.com
Page 112

WestCoast ParkCenter Suites
424 East ParkCenter Boulevard
Boise, Idaho 83706
Phone: 208-342-1044
Fax: 208-342-2763
E-mail: sarah.hembree@westcoasthotels.com
www.westcoasthotels.com
Pages 154-155

Index

8th Street, 23, 38
A Christmas Carol, 85
A.C. Green, 86
African-American community, 53
AIDS, 88, 119
Albertson, Joe, 16
Alive After Five, 53
AmeriSuites, 153, 156-157, 162
Ann Morrison Park, 38, 54, 73
Art in the Park, 73, 76
arts, 11, 20, 37, 43, 67, 75, 78, 85, 87-89, 112
Atwood-Hinzman-Jones, 117, 120, 162

Ballet Idaho, 85, 89
Bank of America Center, 88
Barber Dam, 54, 73
basketball, 88
Basques, 53-54
bass, 55, 134
Beaux Arts, 85
black history, 38, 43, 88, 99
Blue Cross of Idaho, 141, 146-147, 162
Bogus Basin Ski Resort, 83, 88
Bogus Basin, 37, 83, 88, 93
Boise Art Museum, 37, 43, 73, 76, 85, 158
Boise Cascade, 18, 101
Boise Center, 85
Boise City Arts Commission, 87
Boise Contemporary Theater, 75, 78
Boise Heart Clinic, 141, 150, 162
The Boise Master Chorale, 85
The Boise Metro Chamber of Commerce, 2, 5, 9, 11, 105, 110-111, 132, 162
Boise Philharmonic, 75
Boise Rescue Mission, 85
Boise River, 16, 22, 37, 54, 63, 69-70, 73, 81, 111, 154, 159
Boise State Pavilion, 88
Boise State University (BSU), 27, 35, 37, 40, 47, 73, 102, 110, 121-122
The Bon Marché, 153, 158-159, 162
Boy Scouts, 85, 109

Bronco Stadium, 74, 86, 121
Bruneau Sand Dunes State Park, 40, 70
BSU Pavilion, 37
Building Materials Holding Corporation, 97, 101, 162
Bureau of Reclamation, 16

Caldwell, 27, 54, 144
camping, 20, 70
Canyon County, 54, 74
Capitol Boulevard, 38, 162-163
Capitol building, 87, 122
Cascade, 18, 55, 101
CH2M HILL, 117, 121, 162
Cherry Festival, 54
Christmas, 85-86, 90
Cinco de Mayo, 35, 40
City of Light Women and Children's Shelter, 86
the City of Trees, 6, 9, 15-16, 18, 33, 37, 40, 47, 70, 86, 88
Civil War, 16
climate, 6, 11, 18, 53, 55, 59, 81
CM Company, Inc., 127, 139, 162
community education classes, 87
Community House, 85
construction, 7, 9, 15-16, 21, 70, 101, 118, 122, 124, 127-131, 136-139, 163
crappies, 55

Dairy Days, 54
Davis, Thomas Jefferson, 16
Daylight Savings Time, 53
Deli Days, 53
DIRECTV Boise Customer Contact Center, 97, 100, 162
Discovery Center, 37, 43, 113
downtown, 9, 16, 18-20, 37, 44, 53-54, 56, 60, 65, 83, 85, 99, 110-111, 113, 120, 131, 142, 145-146, 148-149, 154, 158-159, 161

Eagle, 54, 59, 106, 113, 124, 128, 130, 163
Easter, 40
Emmett, 54, 56, 122, 150
entertainment, 6, 11, 40, 53-56, 65, 70, 78, 85, 100, 154-155
Extended Systems, 18

F&C Corporation and Rocky Mountain Management & Development, LLC, 127, 138, 162
Festival of Trees, 85, 114, 144
fine arts, 88
fireworks, 54
First Night celebration, 87
floating, 54
Food Bank, 85
food drives, 85
football, 20, 73-74, 86, 130
foothills, 6, 9, 15-16, 20, 39-40, 53, 55, 65, 70, 85, 88, 110
French trappers, 16
fun run, 20

Garden Valley, 55, 85
Gem State, 70, 87, 123
Gene Harris Jazz Festival, 40, 47
golf, 20, 59, 154
government, 16, 19, 87, 110-111
Great West Casualty Company, 105, 114, 162
Greek Festival, 53
Greenbelt, 22-23, 37-38, 70, 111, 154
Grove plaza, 53

habitec, 117, 124, 129, 131, 162
Handel's *Messiah*, 85
handicrafts, 55-56, 88
Harry Morrison, 16
Hawks, 56, 63
Hawley Troxell Ennis & Hawley LLP, 117, 123, 162
health care, 7, 11, 19, 85, 141, 146-147, 150-151
Hewlett-Packard, 18, 97-98, 162

higher education, 19
hiking, 20, 70
"H" Bowl, 86
hockey, 88
Holiday Parade, 85
Holland & Hart LLP, 117-118, 162
horse racing, 20
HP Women's Challenge, 39, 56
Humanitarian Bowl, 86
hunting, 20, 81
Hyde Park, 38, 65

Idaho Anne Frank Human Rights Memorial, 23
Idaho Black History Museum, 38, 99
Idaho Center, 56
Idaho City, 55, 70, 88
Idaho Ice World, 88
The Idaho Shakespeare Festival, 33, 56, 113
Idaho's first billionaire, 18
Independence Day, 55-56
Intermountain West, 87

Jai Aldi, 54
Jazz, 40, 47, 56-57
Jewish community, 40
John L. Scott Real Estate, 87, 127, 134-135, 163
Johnson, Kevin, 86
Julia Davis Park, 37, 43, 57, 67, 73, 76
Juneteenth, 53

Karen Louise Fashion Boutique, 153, 161, 163
kayakers, 55
KeyBank, 105, 113, 163
Knudsen, Morris Hans, 16

Lake Lowell, 55, 74
lakes, 55
Lawmakers, 16, 87
Leatham-Krohn-Van Ocker, Architects, 117, 122, 163

Les Bois Park, 44, 55
les bois, 16, 44, 55, 63
little league, 38
Log Cabin Literary Center, 87
Lucky Peak State Park, 55

McCall, 55, 70, 85, 88
McDonald's, 18
medicine, 87, 142-143, 150
Meridian, 7, 54, 56, 85, 106, 108, 122, 131, 137, 139, 146, 149-150, 153, 160, 162-163
Meridian Ford, 153, 160, 163
Micron Technology, 18, 28, 102
Morrison, Ann, 38, 54, 73
Morrison-Knudsen Company, 16
Morrison Center for the Performing Arts, 37, 75, 87, 89
mountain biking, 20, 39
mountain towns, 88
Music Week, 40, 47

Nampa, 27, 54, 75, 106, 122
Nampa's Civic Center, 75
New Year, 87
Night Lite, 54
Night Rodeo, 54
Nordic skiers, 88
North End, 11, 38, 65
The Nutcracker, 85, 89

Opera Idaho, 75
operas, 40
Oregon, 16, 28, 87, 106-107, 121, 134, 138, 142, 150, 158
Oregon Trail, 16

parks, 11, 19, 24, 54, 65, 72-73, 122, 124
Passover, 40
Payette River, 55, 87

Perch, 55
Peregrine Fund, 81
Petra, 127, 136-137, 163
Plunkett, Jim, 86
Portland, 16, 87, 134, 138-139
potatoes, 28
prose and poetry, 87

Race to Robie Creek, 38, 49
rafters, 55
raptors, 70
recreational opportunities, 9, 18-19, 24
Regence BlueShield of Idaho, 141, 151, 163
regional commerce, 19
restaurants, 38, 53, 88, 124, 129, 131
River Festival, 54, 159
River Giants Parade, 54
Rodriguez, Chi Chi, 86

Saint Alphonsus Regional Medical Center, 55, 85, 141-142, 163
St. Luke's Regional Medical Center, 7, 19, 85, 141, 147-148, 150, 163
Saint Patrick's Day, 40
Saints Constantine and Helen's Church, 53
Salt Lake City, 16, 87
scenic drives, 55
Shaefer's Butte, 37
Silver City, 60, 70
Simplot, Jack, 18
Simplot Agribusiness, 18
ski resort, 20, 83, 88
skiing, 9, 20
Snake River Birds of Prey National Conservation Area, 70
Snake River Stampede, 54, 56
snow, 6, 9, 16, 37, 81, 85-86, 93
snowboarders, 83, 88
snowmobiling, 20
soccer, 20, 38, 59, 73
softball, 53

soul food, 53, 67
Stanley, 55
State Capitol, 15-16, 37, 122
Steed Construction, 21, 127-131, 163
Steelheads, 88
Sun Valley, 55

Temple Ahaveth Beth Israel, 53
tennis, 38, 53
Thanksgiving, 54, 75, 85
Jefferson Davis, Thomas, 16
Thornton Oliver Keller, 38, 127, 132-133, 163
Time Warner Telecom, 97, 102, 163
Towne Square Mall, 85, 130, 158
transportation, 19, 28, 110-111, 122, 145, 156
Treasure Valley, 6, 15-16, 24, 27, 56, 67, 70, 88, 109-110, 114, 121-122, 124, 128, 134, 137-139, 142, 144, 151, 160
Trout, 37, 55

United Heritage, 73, 105-109, 163
Utah, 87, 106, 118

Valentines, 88
Velma Morrison Interpretive Center, 70, 81

Wells Fargo, 105, 112, 163
West Coast Hockey League, 88
WestCoast ParkCenter Suites, 154-155, 163
Western Athletic Conference, 86
whitewater rafting, 20
winery, 56-57
World Center for Birds of Prey, 70, 81
The World Sports Humanitarian Hall of Fame, 86

Zoo Boise, 37, 43, 74, 113